CW01662273

MEXTED
Pieces of Eight

MEXTED
Pieces of Eight

with Alex Veysey

Rugby Press Limited
Auckland

© Rugby Press Ltd
First published in 1986 by
Rugby Press Ltd
P.O. Box 37-291, Parnell, Auckland, New Zealand

ISBN 0-908630-25-5

Typesetting and design
by Harlen Graphics Auckland
Cover design by Ray Bolderson
Printed by Kyodo-Shing Loong Printing Ltd, Singapore

No part of this publication may be reproduced or transmitted in any form or by any means electronic or mechanical, including photocophy, recording or any information storage retrieval system without permission in writing from the publisher.

Dedicated to my father, Graham

Acknowledgements

The publishers extend their special thanks to Wellington photographer Peter Bush, so many of whose outstanding pics, colour and black and white, appear in this book.

Special thanks also to the following photographers, agencies and newspapers who have allowed their photos to be used:

Agence Presse-Sports, Paris; *France Soir*, Paris; Mike Brett, London; *Evening Post*, Wellington; Ross Setford, Auckland; Green and Hahn, Christchurch; *Dominion*, Wellington; *Citizen*, Johannesburg; Ron Cooke, Taumarunui, Wessel Oosthuizen, Johannesburg.

Contents

Foreword

No one could deny Murray Mexted has lived life in the fast lane, a devout adherent to the philosophy of the Spoofers society to which he belongs: "Life is not a rehearsal . . ."

Yet within that context he has been able to build himself a reputation among his fellow players as, perhaps, the most intense team man of them all.

In a country as devoted to rugby and as steeped in its tradition as New Zealand it is not possible to play in 34 successive test matches as a forward (and all as No. 8) without having exceptional qualities. Yet Murray Mexted's remarkable record and, with it, his devotion, has not always won unreserved acclaim. There are those who do not share his passionate approach and there are those who have regarded his black-white-and-no-grey attitude as something beyond the pale. But as one of the game's fiercest competitors he takes his honesty on the field to his life off it and he has a compelling urge to reject platitude.

He has become so saturated in the pride of the title "All Black" that the responsibility it carries with it is a consuming passion. That is only one of the reasons he is a great player. Another is that his instinct for the game was honed to such sharpness that, combined with his competitiveness and his athleticism, it carried him clear of pretenders to his position since 1979.

The rampaging athlete which was Mexted in his early years has become the mature player blending his own special talent into team requirements, into a ball-distributing role in which he has few equals in world rugby. Few forwards are so frequently found playing a handling part in so many scoring movements. It is a quality which too often has escaped attention and appreciation.

It is tempting to reach for superlatives to describe a comrade in a piece such as this but I find the Mexted playing record sufficient justification for what, applied to a lesser player, might appear to be exaggeration.

Murray's strong individual streak may seem to eliminate the very basis of success in a team sport. But in close association with those principle in his sector of the game — especially Dave Loveridge and Mark Shaw — he has played a strong hand in achieving superb team-function.

Not all who have played with Murray claim great affinity with him but few deny that to be in his team is infinitely better than to have him in opposition — and that realisation in itself is an endorsement both of his ability and his loyalty to his team-mates.

His book is a broad-ranging coverage of a career in and out of rugby which has brought his life a unique style. No one has more enjoyed the peripheral possibilities of international rugby. The opportunities it offers for travel have transported him to the game's many corners. Its commercial connections have activated his business inclinations. Its social atmosphere, second to none in sport, has rubbed off on one of rugby's most adventurous socialisers . . . a spoofer, a surfer and formerly a sporting playboy.

To be sure, life is not a rehearsal and no sportsman of my time has so swiftly grasped the need to live it fully as Murray Mexted, All Black.

Andy Haden
Auckland
June, 1986

Fantasy, family, and sawdust

The day the Right Honourable David Lange, Prime Minister of New Zealand, invited me to take my surf board and paddle all the way to South Africa I looked at my beautiful hand-crafted board and thought, "Well, why not?" And I fantasised on the day far hence when the regulars who ride those matchless waves at Jeffreys Bay in the Eastern Cape would shade their eyes and stare far out to sea at the blackened and blistered figure paddling in from the deeps of the Indian Ocean and say without surprise, "Hey, Murray's back" — and carry on surfing.

Not that I'm much given to fantasy. I have lived my life with the philosophy that if it's worth fantasising over it's worth doing. And with a few notable exceptions, such as fulfilling the prime ministerial invitation to paddle to South Africa, I have lived out what some others, less fortunate, would see as impossible dreams.

This has encouraged accusation and commendation in about equal proportions. I have been charged with self-indulgence, arrant professionalism ("how else could he pay his way?"), exotic flamboyance . . . when all I have done is to set myself a course and steer it while still young enough to enjoy it. I cannot quite see the merit, on achieving old age, of looking back on one's youth with dreadful regret that so much was left undone.

Much of what I have done has been spontaneous, without thought to risk-factors or tomorrows. A week before the All Black rugby trial of 1984 I was with some friends paddling a dugout canoe in the Okavango Swamps of Botswana. I got home to play in one of the most memorable rugby weeks of my life, two superb matches, with the New Zealand trial at Hamilton followed by the North-South match at Rotorua. I knew that what I planned between those two matches would have had Pinetree Meads' eyebrows meeting in a calamitous collision had he known — yes, had he known . . .

It had been made plain to me that this week of rugby was something special in my career. No one actually put me in a corner and spelled out to me that not everyone was amused by such flirtations with South Africa that I could arrive home only a few days before an All Black trial. But nor did I need a clairvoyant to define for me that this week was some sort of challenge to front up or play in South Africa. Rather a matter of choice. There never was any shadow of doubt in my own mind, of course. My allegiance to New Zealand rugby and to New Zealand is as fierce as anyone's.

That week there were complications. The day before the trial teams were to assemble in Hamilton there was a beating on the door of the Mexted homestead in Tawa. Two outlandish figures pleaded for recognition. They stood there, hair to their shoulder-blades, beards to their breast-bones. Beneath the hair of one of them was my good friend, Craig Hulett. I had lived with him on the beach at Salt Rock, Natal, and I had always promised that one day I would repay his hospitality.

He and his friend had been surfing about the world for a year. They knew nothing of rugby. The prospect of All Black trials and a match between two islands did not cause them to go into convulsions of ecstasy and anticipation. I explained I was playing in a couple of matches "up country" and suggested they should take my car and surfboard, drive to New Plymouth, have a surf and I would meet them the day of the match in Hamilton.

Things went according to plan. They watched what they judged to be just a casual mid-week game of rugby, joined us for drinks after the game and stayed the night, one sleeping under the stairs, the other in the bed of Bruce Smith, the Waikato winger, who went home after the match.

In fact, what they had watched was the best New Zealand trial I have played in and one which long-experienced rugby-watchers described as one of the finest trial matches there had ever been. Andy Dalton and I skippered the teams, both of which included a surprising number of new players, and I was conscious I had to re-prove myself to the New Zealand selectors just as convincingly as the new boys had to prove themselves. While accepting a player is only as good as his last game I don't necessarily agree it should be seen as an inflexible axiom.

Inevitably in trial rugby there is a strong element of individualism, a built-in requirement in every player's psyche to prove that he, as an individual, has what it takes to become an international player. The over-weighting of trial matches with that sort of mentality as opposed to achieving the impact through being part of a team performance is what turns so many trials into slapdash, incoherent frustrations.

That day at Hamilton was a triumph for a team which had talked through the trial-concept with the coach, Graeme Crossman, formerly an All Black hooker, and agreed that winning well as a team was the only intelligent approach to trial rugby. That may seem a glib conclusion by 15 players thrown together for one of the most important matches of their careers. But the result proved it could be done and it could well be taken as a blueprint by all trial teams.

We had the remarkable boy from Auckland, John Kirwan, scoring three tries in a total of seven, unity in a forward pack committed to forming a platform from which the grand plan could be executed. Where we started off with a man-on-man defence we were able to change smoothly when that threatened disaster with the Manawatu fullback Mark Finlay charging through on the burst. I suggested we start to "drift" and that plugged up the holes and we took such control of the match that we won 36-17.

Dwelling on the background to the event I took personal satisfaction from the swell of team spirit which so swiftly saturated that team and I marvel to this day at the sensational emergence of Bruce Hemara as a hooker-forward worthy of any honour.

The success of that match made what I had to do then a little easier. I am not so brash that I did it with an easy conscience. But there I was with two guests looking to me to provide hospitality and entertainment. It was Wednesday. The North-South match was Saturday. I sweated on the dilemma and persuaded myself that my form was such that I could be excused a little off-field gamesmanship.

I asked our manager, New Zealand Rugby Union councillor Bob Stuart, to tell Colin Meads, the North Island coach, I would be unavailable till Friday. Business reasons, you know. And with my two hirsute visitors I headed for Mt. Maunganui, the beach, the surf and a very fine four-foot wave. Business reasons? Well, funny-business, maybe . . . I didn't really care to rationalise it and the enjoyment of my guests as they hooked into a wave made it worthwhile, anyway.

Rotorua on a rainy day and training in sodden gear on a slippery track was as far removed from Mt Maunganui basking in the sun and soaking in the surf as the Okavango Swamps from Waikiki. But Colin Meads didn't keep us at it long. He saved his shafts for the team-talk, which he attacked with his own agricultural psychology. It was straight-from-the-shoulder King Country with an injection of Fred Allen at his most waspish — not that I ever heard Allen, but his team-talks have become part of rugby folklore.

Pinetree pinned Mark Shaw with a beetle-browned glare, and growled, "You think you're pretty tough." And he paused. And Shaw waited . . . "Well you've never impressed **me** much and they tell me you're even softer this year than you were last . . ."

And he looked directly at me . . . "And **you,** Murray. You're 30 . . ." And he made it sound as if I was passing through a doddery middle-age and entering premature senility . . . "They tell me it's the end of the road at 30. They're saying you've had your day and I can quite believe it . . ."

As we got off the bus at the ground Cowboy Shaw muttered, "He's put it on you and me, hasn't he?" And he went out on to the Rotorua International Stadium and played a blinder. He scored two tries in a tally of five and everything went right for me, too, as North swamped South 39-3.

That wasn't the extent of Meads' input to the game. Far from it. He and Andy Haden, his captain, were perfectly in tune on the strategy of the game and one of the masterstrokes was Meads' treatment of Grant Fox the young Auckland first five-eighths. Meads had demonstrated his confidence in Fox's future the year before when he played him in a North team which, from the point of view of his own credibility as a coach, had to win following a sound defeat by a relatively anonymous South Island team in 1982.

Now Meads quietly told Fox the game was in his hands. He was to call the shots, use the ball as he assessed changing situations. Fox's response was a performance of great maturity and he kicked goals from every try and from three penalties, kicks from as many angles as Pythagoras could dream up in a week.

Late — very, very late — that night Meads and the North Island manager, Peter Wilde, arrived at a great party, their arms around each other, singing. It was not a pretty sound. Meads looked searchingly at my two surfing companions, made his assessment and said, "Gid-day. You'd have to be surfing mates of Mexted's from South Africa. Have a drink." Which they did. And by the end of it all that unlikely threesome were buddies, and the surfies sealed the relationship by calling him not Colin, not Pinetree nor even Piney. To them he was simply Tree.

Great, I thought. I've had my trial, I've had my surfing with my mates and I've had my North-South match and Meads is none the wiser. A coup, my boy, a coup. I learned later — two years later — that Meads

Pinetree Meads . . . the subterfuge was wasted.

knew all. Before Bob Stuart could get to him with my message he held a team meeting. He looked around and asked where I was. Bernie Fraser covered for me. Good old Bernie. "Pinetree," he said, "he's gone to Auckland on a heavy business trip. I know. Because I saw him carrying a briefcase with two fins sticking out of it."

That week led to the selection of All Black teams to play France and to tour Australia and Fiji. No New Zealand selection panel could have wished for a more comprehensive demonstration of total rugby upon which to base their All Black selections. The sort of rugby many trials produce may throw up an extraordinary individual — as, for instance, it did Grahame Thorne in 1967 — but too often trials suffer from too little of the "team" mentality and achieve nothing but embarrassment.

The marrying of individuals of natural talent into combinations and combinations into teams is a skill I was associated with from the time I can remember anything of rugby. I was not conscious of what I was hearing or seeing but the more I watched my father at his training sessions the more I took to myself the nature of the footballers he was coaching.

My father created something of a sensation when he was selected for the All Blacks in 1950 while playing for Tawa, a senior second division club in Wellington. Tawa had one of those gyms you might find in a thousand small suburban clubs — the sawdust floor throwing up that pungent smell which came to mean "rugby" to me. That and the headless draught ale dribbling from the keg in the corner after the match, the snatches of rugby ribaldry, the atmosphere thick with jollification after a key game had been won.

Things impress themselves indelibly on the mind of a six-year-old kid. Players who may never be more than second-division or third-division hopefuls are his towering heroes of the game.

The Whinerays, Tremains, Meadses, the Lineens, Browns, Clarkes were names occasionally heard across the breakfast table, heard but forgotten with the next splash of raspberry jam. The **real** rugby players were named Porky Parata and Rob Solomon and Ken Arthur and Pikau Arthur and Bill Arthur and John Arthur and Richard Thomas and Harold Thomas and . . . every one of those Tawa players had magic in his hands and feet. They could do no wrong. Many of them were Maoris and the flavour of their game was an influence on me even then and in the years which followed.

Their patent enjoyment in running rugby, their delight in having the ball in their hands, their eagerness to abandon formality if the same result could be achieved with half a dozen sidesteps, a looping over-

As it was in the beginning . . . Tawa Midgets, 1963. Ball-carrier Mexted sole playing survivor 23 years later.

head pass or a dummy to someone who wasn't there at all . . . these things my father Graham took to himself as bonuses rather than rigidly squeeze his Maori players dry of fun and expressiveness.

So at six, with sawdust between my toes and up my nose, I was learning a part of rugby I have never forgotten, not by studying or consciously watching and listening to learn, but by always being there, and absorbing it all into my bones and my heart.

Tawa has been in the bones and hearts of many Mexteds. I am a sixth generation New Zealander, descendant of the Maxteds, as they then were, who came to Port Nicholson in the Lord William Bentinck in 1841, the 17th immigrant ship to arrive in New Zealand and only the second in Wellington. George and his family settled in the Johnsonville area. He was a Kentish man of the land, an agricultural labourer when he emigrated and within a few years of settling, a farmer and land-owner.

So from 1841 there has been a Mexted presence in the Johnsonville-Tawa area, but it was Tawa that became home. There has always been a vigorously-flowing current of family pride and patriotism in the Mexteds. I know of no more patriotic New Zealander than my father — assertively proud of his country not only in rugby but in all its achievements. It has washed over all of us.

I was Gary Mexted for a week. The first week of my life. The day I was born my father helped Wellington defend the Ranfurly Shield against Auckland. By the time I became Murray he knew he had missed selection in the All Blacks to tour Great Britain and France. His had been an astonishing introduction to international rugby.

He was an outstanding all-rounder at Wellington College, a tennis champion, a track champion — but never in the first XV. He played for Wellington College Old Boys in 1944-45-46, making the Wellington fourth grade reps as a centre in 1944 and then playing centre, wing or full-back for the club third-graders, juniors and seniors.

District allegiance called in 1947 when the Tawa club was formed. It marched from junior second division, to junior first and, in 1950, into the senior second division. Dad played in the forwards only because that was where the club was at its thinnest.

That year the Lions toured. He was plucked out of Tawa and sent off to Blenheim with Wellington B and the next Saturday was no. 8 in the Wellington team which lost 6-12 to the Lions. On July 1, he has told me, he was sitting on the old Western Bank at Athletic Park watching one of the most inspiring performances by a New Zealand pack, a pack reduced by injury and transfer to the backs, to six players . . . "If anyone had said to me then," he said, "that I would be playing in the fourth test at Auckland in three weeks time I'd have said, 'you're bloody mad'."

But he was. G.G. Mexted, Tawa second division, one game for Wellington B, two games for Wellington A, Western Bank viewer of the third test, All Black No. 8 for the fourth, then in 1951 an All Black tour of Australia. Fairy-tale stuff for a kid from Tawa.

G.G. always said he took his ball skills from his father, who was good at anything he turned his hand to but never a competitor as we know competition. I have vivid memories of Cecil Champion Mexted, my grandfather. Dad has told me of his vitality and his strength — a 150lb bag of grain under one arm and a 200lb bag of pollard under the other — and also of his gentleness. As a small boy I dissolved under his irreverance, gales of helpless laughter at the dinner table as he devoutly put his hands together, stared solemnly toward Heaven and recited: "Dearly beloved brethren, is it not a sin/ That when you peel potatoes you throw away the skin/ For the skin feeds the pig and the pig feeds you/ Dearly beloved brethen, is that not true?"

And if you think that lacks religious sincerity before a fine meal, try his other favourite line, intoned with sonorous gravity over a Sunday lunch: "Lord, I have followed you for seven days without changing my socks." And always followed by a quizzical glance at the kids — enough to make a six-year-old laugh till his belly hurt, and cry because he

My All Black father, Graham, obliges the press immediately following my New Zealand selection.

couldn't stop laughing.

He and my grandmother started their married life with £250. The depression slayed them as they tried to build a business with three hard-tyred trucks. He was a farmer's son and he knew about hard work. He contracted to cart all the milk from the district into Wellington and he developed that into general carrying while he was still milking cows himself. He bought a garage with a Plume pump, he had his sons, Brian and Graham, loading and unloading tonnes of native timber for delivery from railhead to sawmills, timber so green my father reckons the birds still sang in it.

When Dad left school he was going to make a handsome living even if it did mean going to Varsity to study for an accountancy degree. My grandfather observed that exercise, not with contempt, but with a half-amused tolerance that anyone could be so short-sighted that he would study to earn less than his truck drivers. On reflection, Dad judges that as a cunning stratagem, designed to pull the boys into the business. It worked.

My grandfather laid the dirt upon which the Tawa Rugby Club was built and if only for that one act he would have left a legacy to thousands of kids who have honed their rugby wits on that patch of ground. My childhood fun was often working-fun with him, running about like a beaver, cleaning up the rubbish of the day's work, surrounded by men doing men's work while I pretended to be one of them, then dashing off to Lyndhurst Park to kick a ball over — or at — the posts. Four points for a dropped goal, three for a placekick, two for a punt and one for a catch.

Cecil Champion, for all his gentleness and humour, did not come easily to terms with dramatic shifts in lifestyle; mechanical or technical change from the old ways sometimes caught him unawares and on those occasions his reaction was hairtrigger stuff. Like the day he rushed into Mexted Motors in Tawa, found Dad on the phone, grabbed his car keys, said, "I'm just taking your car for a while," and rushed out again. He hopped into the car, a 1958 Plymouth Belvedere — push-button automatic. He started it, revved up, grabbed the indicator stalk on the steering column, tried to ram it into gear and wrenched it right off. He stormed out of the car and into Dad's office, hurled the indicator stalk on his desk and yelled in blind frustration, "Stick that up your arse." Dad, normally an obedient son, didn't. My grandfather never did really trust push-button automatic transmission after that.

I was given rugby boots on my fifth birthday and slept with them. I guess that was the real beginning of it. As a student I worked as hard as I needed to. I didn't slack, though sometimes there seemed more important things to do. Tawa Primary School had educated my father and my grandfather. When I was in the classroom I was aware there was a heap of open, green ground out there. I did not regard teachers as ogres or slave-drivers but there were times when they did seem to be over-insistent in matters of detail, homework and getting your work done before you got out to play footy or cricket.

When I was 11 I was a king. I played on Athletic Park for the Western Bays primary schools representatives. It was one of those miserable, windblown, wet days Wellington has so very occasionally but I didn't care. And I didn't care even less when I scored a try. The only hiccup to my total rapture over the whole occasion was when the referee disapproved of what I reckoned, at the age of 11, to be a staggering piece of innovative rugby. We had a scrum under our posts, the city half-back to feed it and a try on. Playing number eight for the Bays I saw the city hooker do his part and the ball was travelling through devious channels but emphatically on its way to their number eight and, inevitably from him to the half-back. I pulled my head out, climbed on to our locks, crawled over the front rows, over their locks and grabbed the ball as it came out from the number eight.

The referee didn't blow the whistle. He stared at me for several seconds. Then he laughed a bit, blew his whistle and said, "You can't do that lad," and penalised me. I didn't feel I had quite the background to go into an academic discussion on the rules but I did feel a little hard-done by. If, from time to time, you detect some slight expression of dissent from me over a test referee's decision, you may now understand that my suspicions of referees are long-standing and deep-seated.

I played on "The" Park later for the Wellington primary reps and, much later, for the Wellington secondary school reps but nothing matched that first time till I had my first international there — and for the sheer joy of playing on the ground maybe even that did not equal the primary school days.

Much happened to my rugby through those years and in the years immediately following. I loved my intimacy with the Tawa Club. We were next-door neighbours physically and in the days when social graces were such that keys were seen to be irrelevant to life it became my second home. I remember nothing of my father's influence on my rugby — yet he was the greatest influence of all just by allowing me to be there, to absorb the atmosphere of a club and to develop my love for rugby through the characters who played for him and through the character of the rugby they played.

He always told me I was dead lucky to have the mother I had. If he had married someone else, he said, I would never have been the sportsman I was. I'm not too sure of the genetic logic of that but I know what he meant. My mother, Beverley, was an outstanding athlete as a girl and young woman. She went to school to play sport, lived for it no matter whether it was basketball, tennis, swimming, acrobatic diving, athletics, badminton . . .

She won the inter-collegiate high jump championship as a western-roller and taught me that technique to win the intercollegiate title with 5ft 8in in 1971. What she gave to me she also gave to my sisters Sherry and Marilyn and to my brother Alan for they all have uncommon sporting ability.

Nor did she believe in coercing her children into a way of life which had no appeal for them . . . "You are free spirits," she said, and I eagerly took that to myself.

Athletically, I suppose I was hyperactive. Specialisation? No way. I liked to jump and run and throw the discus. A sprint or a middle distance? Run both. At rugby training I could not slow down. During those round-the-paddock warmup jogs I sprinted. I suppose props and locks considered this as untoward exhibitionism but I could never resolve the theorem that slowly-slowly catchee monkey.

Though I had a go at everything nothing matched rugby. Dad never said, "You've **got** to play" or "You **should** play". All my first clues came from those team-talks and what have become rugby cliches — some of them I think coined by Bill Freeman, now coaching director for the New Zealand Rugby Union . . . "Kick to land, not to hand; kick to make ground, pass to score tries. What is the best thing I can be doing for my team at this moment? If you don't make the first tackle you might as well not play the game . . ."

Just as my grandfather used to take the Tawa team Dad played in to their games in his canopy-truck so did my father run the family wheels to aid the team he coached. Most of the Maori players came from the Porirua Pa and he picked them up and dropped them off in his big old V8. The Maoris' approach rubbed off on to me lastingly. I am sure my swift affection for the French game had its seeds in what I saw and heard at Tawa in those far-off days.

Sometimes Dad observed with bemusement my fly-by-night peregrinations in later life. He had played rugby because it was the thing to do. The other thing to do was set a base for your life. People didn't have the means to go ski-ing or surfing or rugby-playing around the world. But he never interfered — just as he had never forced his way on me in my rugby. Here he was, an All Black number eight with a son striving to make his way in the same postition. I am aware of his attitude. He had seen too many cases of top rugby players, including All Blacks, pushing their sons to achieve — an activity, he says, which quickly breeds resentment and withdrawal.

He had learned his rugby the hard way — PT on the gravel road outside the Tawa Fire Brigade and beer in the backroom of the butcher's shop because the butcher was the club captain . . . I was in a different ball-game.

The most crucial lesson I learned from my father was one he had learned from Bill Freeman. He asked Freeman to come and watch a certain player of the Tawa team, to give his judgment of his ability. At the end of the game Freeman said to Dad, "How many times did he get the ball in hand?" Dad said he had no idea. Freeman said, "Twice in the first spell and three times in the second."

When Dad passed that on it was to impress on me that the selector watches only the one player who may be on the verge so I couldn't be cruising around in my lower-grade trial matches. "You must play," said my father, "as if someone is watching only you **all** the time."

There are lessons within the lesson and they benefit rugby as a game for the players and a game for the spectators. The spectators must take something away from the ground, something they can talk about and reflect on with enjoyment. To give it to them the players in my teams will play the sort of rugby they, too, enjoy . . . preferably we will not kick the ball out; preferably we will not allow the ball to die in the tackle. We will try to do something which will keep everyone in top gear and that can be done by keeping the ball alive. Tactically, the line has to be drawn somewhere but where a situation is not critical these things must be our concern.

OE — and other growing pains

Just as my father was plucked out of a so-called "obscure" lower division club to play for Wellington and then put under pressure to change clubs, so was I. There was some measure of ultimatum in his case, none in mine. He was told, along with his Tawa half-back Vince Bevan, that if he was to be considered for the Wellington representatives he should play for a senior first division club. That was put to him by the sole selector Norman Millard — even though both Dad and Vince had been recent All Blacks. Both went to Vince's former club, Athletic.

My move was more under persuasive suggestion. In 1973 Jack Oldershaw picked me for the Wellington second and third division representatives. That was sufficient surprise for me. But then he told me he wanted me to captain the side when, realistically, I considered I would be a reserve. My surprise showed. He asked me if I thought I couldn't handle it. I had that surge of panic that comes when, from a distance, you see your midfield breached and the tryline open and you know you're too far away to do a damn thing about it. I corner-flagged like hell and told him, yes, I could handle it.

I was playing for the Tawa third division team, number eight and off the back of the lineout. The number eight position in the lineout appealed to me only because it gave me the perfect start to move quickly into the game's action. I didn't want to play anywhere that would curb even minutely my need to be in the play. I have this feeling that enthusiasm and energy are under-rated qualities, that they are a marvellous launching pad from which sophistication will develop.

The second and third division team played Wellington B at Athletic Park. Trevor Snowden captained Wellington B and to me, still lean though tall, he looked a giant. His sweatband corrugated his brows, he had just taken a slow bath in linament and he had splattered a vat of vaseline over his brows and nose. He glowered when we crunched hands just to emphasise that shaking hands was a matter of enmity not a gesture of amiability.

But all it meant to me was big-time. All I could think was, "Shit! This is it! I've cracked it! I've arrived!" Which was an extraordinary expression of optimism from a second and third division novice, aged 20, wet behind the ears and not given to bathing in linament.

So there was the precocious kid Mexted flying higher than an angel-dust addict in 1973. That would seem to presuppose there would be frenetic preparation for 1974 — intensified training for stamina and speed, weights to pump up biceps, triceps, quadriceps, pectorals, abdominals, deltoids, laterals, medials and any other muscles great or small identified in the Bodybuilder's Guide to Incredible Hulkritude. And, of course, there would be improvement of the mind — reading into the small hours Fred Allen on Rugby, Rugger — the Man's Game, The Art of Rugby Football — anything to sharpen the understanding of motivation, tactics, assorted man-management techniques . . .

So I would, obviously, be doing all those things. But this was not 1950-something or even 1960-something. It was 1973 and the height of the mad OE era. Everyone worth his salt had to find some OE and I wanted mine badly. Overseas Experience is one of the truly great euphemisms. It implies that young people sweat to save the money to go abroad to the mecca appropriate to the furtherance of their profession or calling and there, by more sweat, absorb the advanced technology which will enable them to go back home so highly qualified that no job is good enough for them.

Our sort of OE was going to be something rather removed from that. "We" were Graham Archer, one of life's good companions, a rugby player of repute if not renown, and Bruce Good. In London we lived in a state of wild schizophrenia. Two of us worked our days in the East End while the three of us lived our nights to the full in the West End. The plan was to work — hard if need be — during the day, play heavily by night and have our rugby on Saturday.

In our job search I filled in a form claiming I was an accountant — an appalling piece of misrepresentation. My technique was to look young and puzzled and say, "Oh, but we don't do it this way at home," have a system described to me and, using animal cunning, get the job done. It worked for a couple of months, too, until some ambitious accounts clerk noted that on one job I was not merely puzzled over technqiue

I was hopelessly lost in this haystack of figures. They didn't actually have the heavies hurl me into the snow. They invited me with charm to consider other work elsewhere.

"Elsewhere" turned out to be the London Linen Supply. Instead of driving a calculator I drove an eight-ton truck in streets an inch or two narrower than an eight-ton truck. That, of course, took incredible skill. Each truck had a driver and a "boy". The boy was aged anywhere between 15 and 60 and he called the driver "guv'nor".

My "boy" came to work with beautifully polished shoes and pressed jeans and a ragged scar from the inside of his left eye across the cheek to the bottom of the chin. "Knife," he told me laconically just a few days before he pulled one on me because I got impatient and yelled at him. To me, the flick-knife made a noise like a door slamming even in the hubbub of a mid-London sidestreet. Probably, it was a gesture of bravado. Somehow, his eyes didn't seem to be in it. I stepped toward him instinctively, eyeball to eyeball, and the blade switched back.

That was some sort of water-shed in our relationship. He became my closest ally. My minder. Then one day the police came and took him away.

He had told me in the morning. "They'll be coming for me. I had this fight on the tube. Tossed this guy on the lines. I wanted him run over, the bastard." When they came for him he went quietly, with resignation.

His replacement was a big ox of a man from Trinidad. I've seen some strong men in action but he was something else. He could do with one hand what would take Gary Knight two. And his swearing was awesome. Somehow he could break words of one syllable with a four-letter descriptive, and I would defy even Grizz Wyllie to do **that** in a team talk.

The "boys" couldn't understand us. Each morning we arrived in East End London in a new leased car — a Hillman Hunter which eventually we drove, 23,000 miles around Europe. We were creatures from another planet. We talked funny, we drove a car from the West End to the East End to work and we had hair down to our chests. We drove these trucks sufficiently well to win their respect — though it took me a couple of bent lamp-posts and a flattened MG before I could rear-mirror reverse in those alleys with confidence.

After a while I became the London Linen Supply's debt-collector in my delivery area as well. For the first week or so I was a sucker for a hard-luck story. Restaurant and bed-and-breakfast proprietors rubbed onions in their eyes just before I arrived, called all their kids around, wrung their hands and told me in half a dozen different dialects that things were real crook. It was all too much for a soft-hearted kiwi. Then I woke up to the intelligence that one thing a restaurant-owner cannot afford is a disturbance in his eating-house. Next time I got the hard-luck story I walked into the crowded cafe and dumped a piled-up laundry basket in the middle of a table. Glasses smashed, soup spattered, curry-and-rice made satisfying puddles on the floor. I was half-way through saying, "Oh, gosh, I'm sorry about that" when suddenly I had a handful of money and a solicitous usher to the door. Word spread and things got easy.

But where to play rugby? We had no connections so we stopped a well-dressed chap in the street and asked where the nearest footy club was . . . "When you say **'footy',** old boy . . ." and he looked distressed at having to use the word . . . "When you say **'footy',** old boy, I'm taking it you actually mean rugby. Rugby union. **Rugger.**"

That, we assured him, was a perfect interpretation, spot-on don't you know. And he directed us to Rosslyn Park. We wandered in, looking lost and very colonial. Somehow, with incredibly swift sleight of hand, this bloke we'd never seen had large glasses of ale in our hands and was telling us how jolly welcome we were. And we were. It was typical of British rugby — immediate concern, warmth of attention and a couple of pints of best bitter.

Arch was slotted into the third team and I into the fourth and we went our separate ways. It was a good game for me. There were two tries and a caution for over-vigorous play. Arch had a good game and was invited to play for the second team. I was invited to stay in the fourths. Again we both played pretty well. Arch was invited to join the first team for the match against Oxford University. I was invited to stay in the fourths. I wondered whether I should change my cologne.

We were both delighted for Arch. So delighted that we celebrated with monumental indifference to time and tide. Arch awoke, decidedly on the gruesome side, groaned with anguish when he could read the time, rushed around for shorts and jock-strap, heaved himself out of the flat, got on a tube, got off a tube at an appropriate place to be unwell, got on another tube and finished up somewhere far removed from Oxford.

The next week he was invited to play for the second team. I was invited to play for the fourths. It seemed odd in that the standard down there was not high and we deemed it time for some ego-massage: Sunday rugby and a bloody good time. We joined Sunday Variety. That meant that we met every Sunday at the White Swan, Richmond, for drinks with the opposition and the referee — three pints while we philosophised grandly and watched the swans on the river. Then off to the game.

Our team was full of Irishmen, Scotsmen, Englishmen, plus a New Zealand shearer, an Aussie and us. If that seems an unlikely mix I can assure you those Sunday matches, their preliminaries and their aftermaths, comprised in one package the sheer joy of playing rugger in England.

My joy stopped short one Sunday afternoon. I was playing fullback and was hit fore and aft with simultaneous tackles. Something appalling happened inside my right knee.

When the cruciate ligaments rupture, doctors told me, you may one day play a game of rugby again or you may play 101 or 10001. **You,** regrettably, will not play again. So what do they know? There will be another doctor, another place. He'll fix it and I'll play. But there was no other doctor in another place who said anything but that my sport was finished. That, of course, was shattering to a young player who, though just fooling around in Sunday games, knew exactly where he wanted to go in rugby.

One day, which I will remember for the rest of my life, someone suggested casually I should go to a sports clinic in London and consult the Chelsea soccer club's physiotherapist. A soccer man? Why not? Soccer players get injured, too. The man gave me confidence immediately. Just by giving me hope. "It could happen," he said. "If you build those quadriceps (the large muscle at the front of the thigh) sufficiently you'll play again. If you're a sidestepper, you'll do that again, too. But it's your pigeon, your self-discipline . . . if you want it badly enough . . ."

I started the sandbag exercises that day, the beginning of what seemed an endless process. One copes with pain. Every man has a different threshhold. More difficult is the retention of hope.

Impatience to see results. Impatience to **feel** results. Those are the killers. And one day you see that the muscle is fattening. And on another you feel that the knee, under stress, responds with more elasticity. You know it's going to happen just as the man from Chelsea said it would. The muscle grows visibly by the day and then you judge it to be twice as big as the one on the left leg and that it is doing the job. And you have to convince yourself it still needs time and that you could destroy it all by taking three pints at the White Swan, philosophising over the swans and saying, OK I'll take the first spell.

OE was not all England. It was Spain, it was Greece, North Africa,

France, Yugoslavia — name it, we went there. To Russia, too, where I learned that a dip in the Volga in mid-winter does one's immediate virility little good but does put a nice hard crease in your jeans. After that particular experience you do not slip out of your jeans, you break them off. Carefully.

That was how I missed the 1974 New Zealand season — with no regrets. And probably it is why OE became almost a way of life for me, much too exhilarating to be a one-off event. I had to go back and back, whether to France, to South Africa — or where ever rugby might take me in search of the different, to renew such friendships which, without rugby, I would never have known. If that made me some sort of nomadic irresponsible in the eyes of those who paddle in the shallows then so be it. What's more, had I been more the orthodox and less the nomad I might never have met my wife — and that seems to me to be the ultimate justification.

In 1975, back with Tawa and loving the challenge of helping to take the club through to senior second division, scoring tries, kicking goals, I was selected for Wellington B — again by Jack Oldershaw who had graduated in the selection stakes. It was a compliment not appreciated by all the senior number eights in the Wellington championship. Paul Quinn, later to be my provincial captain and friend, was sufficiently moved by my selection to front up and tell me he regarded it as a personal insult and that it was an insult, too, to other first division players.

That was not designed to make me feel wanted but my reaction was first of disbelief and then indifference. Things, plainly, were moving for me and I intended helping them along the only way that mattered, by performance.

At that time I was confident on the field but a little diffident off it. Tawa was the beginning of my confidence as a player because with Tawa there was reliance on me to contribute in every way, winning ball, scoring tries, kicking goals, kicking for territory. It was good for my rugby because I was developing all those skills in match conditions. But it was of dubious value to me in the need for concentration on the specific requirements of effective number eight play.

Oldershaw homed in on to this like a stoat on to a lame chicken. At Tawa, he told me, you may do everything. Here, you are to do your job. I suppose I was playing my rugby on instinct and often instinct leads to a self-centred approach which can be disruptive to a planned team pattern. I relate my rugby at that time to the rugby of Geoff Hines, the Tokoroa bushman, who became an All Black on a remarkable raw talent. Geoff just had so much unharnessed pizzaz; he was a rocket and he played like a rocket no matter what team-demands might have been placed on him to pull back into a controlled pattern.

Geoff was naive and so was I. Hadn't I scored 16 tries last season for Tawa down there in senior III? Didn't I know that was the way to go? In his quiet way Jack Oldershaw told me that in his team there was a job for me to do and that must be my focus. Where for Tawa I played off the back of the lineout I was now to play at seven — and with that, Oldershaw created a whole new career for me.

My first game for Wellington B was against Marlborough at Blenheim. That meant Murray Mexted (Tawa, Rosslyn Park 4ths, Sunday Variety XV) 6ft 4, 13½ stone versus Alan Sutherland (All Black, 64 matches, 10 tests and 157 points for New Zealand) 6ft 3, 16 stone. If that sounds like a scenario for disaster I was not really conscious of it. I was too naive to be concerned. My first game for Wellington B, marking Alan Sutherland; great, beauty, funtime. I didn't know enough to be worried.

I didn't mind, either, being taught the lessons Sutherland taught me in that game. They would be useful to me one day — as in my first game for Wellington A, against another hard-nosed veteran named Wyllie . . .

Marlborough threw into the first lineout. Sutherland stepped back. I didn't know why. I just thought, well, here's a bonus, a free go. I was balancing for that perfect, soaring, symmetrical leap to the ball. I could feel already the slap of leather in both hands and see the perfect delivery to the half-back. Sutherland? He had to be a mug giving me all that space. The ball was in the air, my timing was immaculate — I could sense everything right. What I got was a shove in the back from the biggest hand in world rugby. The classical leap became a comedy. I stumbled into the back of my skipper, Trevor Morgan, went down on a knee, grabbed someone to pull myself up, pulled him off balance . . . God, how embarrassing. Meanwhile, that mug Sutherland was in the air, taking the ball two-handed, delivering it, unimpeded, to his half-back and by the time I had unravelled a few legs and arms it was out into the centres.

Next lineout. Marlborough's throw. Sutherland steps back. Mexted steps back. Sutherland shuffles back a shade further. So does Mexted. It's like a hoe-down. Sutherland's eyebrows go up and he nods. The lesson has been delivered and absorbed.

At the last lineout of the game Mexted chances his arm and his life. He catches Sutherland unprepared, shovels him out of the lineout, takes the ball, delivers it and heads off at remarkable speed as Sutherland

Alan Sutherland, right . . . first lessons from an expert. Beside him is his brother Ray.

seeks retribution. Whistle. End of game. Showers all round. When a Wellington administrator asks Sutherland what he thinks of the young "up-and-coming" number eight Sutherland is lavish in his praise. "Well," he says reluctantly, and pauses, "at least he's got some height."

In that, at least, Sutherland and I are on a wave-length. His comment was pregnant with meaning. At this stage of my career little gives me as much pleasure as noting short number eights selected for provincial teams. Realistically and without conceit, that means my position in the All Blacks is less at risk. I have immense regard for players like Dale Atkins, Alan Dawson, Wayne Shelford as footballers. They are tigerish, strong men and they have skill. For all his rugby with Canterbury Dale Atkins is still a young man . . . but none is tall enough to be a number seven lineout jumper in international rugby.

If that sounds simplistic it is because it is a simple truth. Number seven is a possession-winning spot, invaluable.

"New-style" number eights have been coming and going throughout my career. I refer to "new-style" to distinguish between the traditional New Zealand requirement on the number eight — the corner-flagging zealot — and the broad demands on him now. Graham Mourie, I believe, created the "new-style" number eight and he opened up a whole new world of close-support, ball-carrying opportunities for me.

When I first went to play for the French club Agen in 1977 I was 23 with a New Zealand trial behind me. I did not know Mourie well but out of the blue I received a telephone call from Paris where Mourie was playing with Paris University. He was coming south-west he said, to spend the weekend in Auch at the chateau of his friend Jean Le Droff, who had locked the French scrum against Wilson Whineray's All Blacks in 1964 . . . "We would like you to come through and join us for dinner."

I was not an All Black. I confess I was excited by Mourie's invitation. I drove to Auch in an old Peugeot 403 and was met by Mourie, his future wife, Claudia, M. Le Droff and his wife. I spoke English and pigeon-French. Mourie spoke pigeon-French and English. Claudia spoke Spanish, pigeon-French and pigeon-English. Le Droff spoke French. His wife spoke Spanish and French. So there was something of a language barrier till we became familiar (to the point of having a passionate love-affair) with the wine of the area and with Armagnac — for Auch is the centre of the Haut-Armagnac region. Then we scaled unheard-of heights of translation and of fluency. What we did not understand we translated with a sort of poetic frenzy which seemed to make everyone happier if not wiser.

The conversation which required no poetry was that which Mourie initiated with me . . . "What do you think the responsibilities of a number eight should be?"

I said: "To give the half-back good ball from the scrum; to be able to win ball at the lineout; to have the speed to cover his backs; to be able to tackle."

Mourie: Where do you reckon the number eight should head after a scrum or a lineout?

Mexted: Behind his backline . . .

And here Mourie defined for me his vision of number eight play.

"The number eight should be the second person to the ball, going forward; not scouting behind his backline, but following the open-side flanker. I have to get to the stage where I **know** you are behind me. If I make the tackle **you** are there to recover the ball. If I pick up the loose ball **you** are there to carry it on. If I go down on the ball **you** are there to go over the top of me. If I force a player to run one way — say, from a lineout — **you** are there to tackle him."

It was a spaced-out scene. I felt strangely as if I was standing off, watching it all happen. And then I felt, "this guy is talking to me as if he knows he will be playing a lot of rugby with me." It was the All Black captain telling me what he expected of me.

His last requirement of a number eight became some sort of symbol of the way we played together. In my first test, against Scotland at Murrayfield two years later, he said, "I'll run wide of Rutherford, try to cut their backs off. That will force him to kick, have a go himself or come back into the forwards."

He warned me John Rutherford was very elusive. But I knew my role. He had enunciated it two years before. It was the second time I had ever gone into a match feeling a specific responsibility to another player at every set phase.

The first time was in the same sort of relationship with Ken Stewart against Argentina earlier that same year and it was aimed at containing Hugo Porta. Till the tests he'd been beating our close defences all around the country. But in the tests we put Stewart on him, backed up by myself, and he was locked up.

I am a believer in natural vibes between players. There was something unreal about the instinctive thought-merging processes between Mourie and myself, Ken Stewart and myself. It has nothing to do with spoken understanding. When I was with Agen I played with a flanker named Christian Lanta. He spoke no English. At that stage I spoke no French. Yet we immediately dropped into a fluent combination. We could not talk about it or plan it. When I tried to speak with him about it he smiled and said, "Rapport, rapport."

With Mourie there emerged options. His reading of a situation, his adaptability, his anticipation opened so many doors. His astonishing capacity to make hair-trigger decisions with the ball in hand brought rugby a bristling new excitement for me. From that point on I was aware of the right alternative at the right time. It has much to do with the senses, much to do with instinct as opposed to experience.

All of which is a far cry from being pushed in the back at Lansdowne Park, Blenheim. But being in that 1975 Wellington B team brought me into direct contact with a player who even before Mourie was an inspiration. Graham Williams, the All Black flanker of 1967-68, did for my commitment to the game what Mourie did for my education. It was Williams who turned me away from Tawa — physically, I emphasise — and toward his own first division club, Wellington.

Oldershaw had said to me, "Murray, you have to play top club rugby next year." But my allegiance to Tawa was strong and I could not imagine going to my Tawa coach, Pikau Arthur, who had been coached by my father when I was a ballboy, and telling him I was leaving the club.

Then Williams told me I would be doing Tawa a favour if I played for the Wellington club for a couple of years and took back to my old club what I had learned . . . "You need consistent top rugby and you can have it with Wellington." I agonised over it, putting off a decision, and then fronted up to Pikau like a deserter.

Two years for Wellington . . . I became so absorbed in the activities of the great club and my rugby took off with such a roar — beyond my dreams — that two years became a rugby-playing lifetime. I never lost my Tawa connection but my life with Wellington became all-consuming. The first year, 1976, I became part of a controversy I wanted no part of, not with my club but with the Wellington representatives.

The year before, the Wellington provincial selector, Ray Dellabarca, had pulled me into his squad a couple of times, had me attend training and sit on the bench for a couple of matches. I supposed he was planning for a 1976 season when he would lose his captain and number eight Andy Leslie to the All Blacks in South Africa. And that, of course, is what happened. But when Andy was available before South Africa Dellabarca selected me as his number eight. And when Andy returned in time for the final match of the season he was not considered.

This was grist for the media mill. Newspapers saw it as a direct snub of the All Black captain and inexcusable. Dellabarca, I think, thrived on a bit of controversy but he also saw me as a good bet for the back

Early days. First year for Wellington Football Club, 1976, v Poneke.

of the lineout. Wellington did not have a good year; there was uncertainty among the players and it seemed the Dellabarca personality grated on some. That led to communication breakdown, lack of confidence. He was innovative and enthusiastic, maybe a better selector than he was a coach. In method he based his coaching on that of Bill Freeman, who had been a highly successful pilot of Wellington rugby, but where Freeman had the unreserved loyalty of his players, here there was sniping and chipping and, sometimes, unpleasantness. In any circumstances it would have been a difficult year for Wellington and Dellabarca believed when he dropped out after that year that he had brought through enough young players to give his successor a good start.

In spite of the nature of the season I tried to make my first full year as a provincial representative pay off as another giant step in my career. With the background of my club rugby with Williams the base was secure. He was a sort of minder in that he sheltered me from the obstruction and aggro which comprise the normal baptism for young players. There were so many good footballers around me. At my first club training a big prop named Peter Rasmussen moved to 6 in the lineout and blocked like a locomotive. "I just **love** blocking," he grinned. With him there and Williams behind I was given a featherbed ride.

Most of all, Williams demonstrated this almost crazed commitment. His quality as a player was, of course, at the highest level but to control the ball he would condemn his body to punishment without question. The ball, he said, was everything. Without it we might as well go home and play ring-a-rosy with the girls next door. A mental picture of Williams and Rasmussen doing that inspires advanced hysteria.

It has been said with truth that baptism by fire for young loose forwards comes in several degrees of heat and that it was not till Stoker (first class) Grizz Wyllie was feeding the flames that the hobs of hell got white-hot. The build-up to my first confrontation with Grizz was not designed to induce blissful slumber. I was pinned in corners everywhere I went by friends and mere acquaintances who fed me with horror stories about Wyllie's appetite for blood.

Graham Williams was captain of the provincial team and I knew I would get fair warning if not sympathy from him. So I asked him how I should handle Wyllie. Williams looked at me as if I were a simpleton. "Look," he said, "it's easy. As the ball goes into the first lineout turn and let him have one."

I considered that. Briefly. "GC," I said, "I don't think that's my style."

"Make it your style for once," he said. "You'll get one back but he'll respect you for it."

Grizz Wyllie . . . stoker (first class) feeding the flames.

Then he added, "Forget it. He's just another player. You play your normal game."

One minute into the game there was a ruck by the touchline. There was an almighty THWACK. The ruck dissolved. Wyllie rose from the bottom of it with murder in his eyes and demanded to know who the four-letter-word had committed the act. Williams said, "I did." Wyllie looked desperately aggrieved. "**You,** Willie," he said in stunned disbelief. "For God's sake, Graham, play rugby will you?" Which, really, would have brought the house down had it been delivered by a slapstick comic. As it had not, there was an element of black comedy in it and no one believed that was the end of it.

The first spell spread itself out nicely for me and I was getting ball back at seven, marking Wyllie. Grizz must have pondered this phenomenon at half-time. It was at the first lineout after the spell that he let his big one go. I had won the ball, a ruck had formed and I was standing in the middle of it, which was a witless thing for me to be doing given the circumstances. It caught me flush on the right ear and had it not been for the equalising effect of the ruck I would have gone down. Quasimodo was swinging on all the bells of Notre Dame right there in the echo-chamber by my eardrum.

The ruck broke up and Graham Williams regarded me with solicitude . . . "OK? I reckon you've got him now. He's obviously getting weaker."

I was thrown no more ball. Al Keown had a feast at the front . . . how that man never became an All Black is beyond me.

On Monday I couldn't hear out of the ear and I was sure something was seriously amiss. The doctor reckoned I'd had wax in my ear for some time and that it had gradually become compounded. I assured him it had been as gradual as a collision with a sledgehammer swung by Arnold Schwarzenegger.

Wyllie has been a mighty rugby player, immensely powerful, fast. They tell me that when he played off the back of the lineout against the Springboks in 1970 he had the South African fly-half, Piet Visagie, scared witless.

I worry, though, about an attitude to the game as it may be expressed through some of the acts of Canterbury on the field. I can speak only of Wellington. When Canterbury took the Ranfurly Shield from Wellington 16-12 in 1982 they removed Allan Hewson from the field with as atrocious an act as I have ever seen committed in the name of sport. Lightweight Hewie had kicked the ball from defence when he was hit grotesquely late by a charging prop who a year before had been his All Black team-mate in the triumph against the Springboks and who had shared in the glory when Hewie had kicked that match-winning goal at Eden Park. I have not forgotten what he did to Hewie at Athletic Park and never will.

And as Wellington exerted pressure in the scrummaging when the game was closely-run Scott Crichton was booted ruthlessly in the head — the sort of act which truly great players through the years have condemned as the ultimate act of viciousness and cowardice.

When Wellington went to Lancaster Park to try to lift the Shield in 1983 our lock Murray Pierce was dominating the lineouts. I cannot recall Pierce perpetrating any ugly misdemeanour in all the matches I have played with him. In this match he literally was taking the shield away from Canterbury in his own two hands. Desperate for Canterbury. So Pierce was removed from the field, his jaw broken by a punch delivered from behind.

I take no pleasure at all in recording these incidents. The game has taken knocks enough. But if some sort of condemnation is not forthcoming in books of this sort it may be seen that players condone what happens on the field, no matter how reprehensible. There must never be a closed-society, a pact of silence, while activities are taking place which bring the game into disrepute.

Rugby is in the process of marketing itself, of presenting itself to the public as the greatest of all sporting entertainments, as a game children want to play and as a game parents want their children to play. One act of mindless violence, taken in a second or two, can destroy months of work in the presentation of the game and whittle away at the historic fibre of the game.

Canterbury plays marvellously efficient rugby; they have players of great skill, many of them good friends of mine. Their Ranfurly Shield record is a matter for immense pride. Their spirit and the nature of their rugby when they cut back Auckland's huge lead in 1985 commands my admiration. It would be shameful were all this healthy expanse of good to be pitted with an acne of disreputable acts by individuals.

It has a spill-over effect, too. If one province, or some of its individuals, are seen to be standing-over their opposition, and gaining profit from it their challengers may well decide the only way to overcome the difficulty is to match fire with fire — and again the image of the game suffers.

Resolute action by referees is a holding action. The prevention is in the hearts and minds of coaches and players. The figures tell the story. There can be no hiding behind "accidental" injury because official evidence is that in 1984 68 per cent of the facial fractures notified by New Zealand unions resulted from foul play . And it is accepted that a higher proportion of facial injuries other than fractures would also result from deliberate acts.

I suppose most of us have been guilty at one time or another of reactive or reprisal action. Yes, I have. There's a particularly unflattering picture of me having a whack at an Argentine player in one of the 1985 tests. And there was that time in Italy . . .

I was playing in South Africa in 1982 when I was invited to go to Italy to play in the Parma club's 50th anniversary match. At a function before the match the Parma president came to me and said, "Today, my friend, you play against my son Giovanni. He is big. He is very big. But he is not hard. He is soft. I so want him to be hard. I want my son to know in himself that he is strong, as strong as an All Black. Will you please compel him to prove that to himself today? You will look after it."

I understood. At the first lineout Giovanni jumped off my shoulder. I gave him a bit of a back-handed swat. A pussy-cat swat. Giovanni blinked sadly and thereafter stood a couple of yards off every lineout. After the game I felt bad about it. I looked the president in the eye. He sighed and heaved his shoulders. He had known, but had sought one last shred of evidence that he was wrong. I hope he is still not putting his boy to one last test.

We have all heard it before and because it has so often been said it is, like all such things, stored away as just another platitude, another cliche: rugby is a great game for character building. Nevertheless, it is true. It enables, **encourages,** the mixing together of young people irrespective of cultural or social backgrounds, irrespective of religion and race. I know of no other activity in this country which achieves what rugby does as a comprehensive social service.

So the game must not be abused by circumstance or design. My club goes back to the beginning of rugby in this country. I have always believed that New Zealand rugby has its special character because it is what we are as people, still so close to our pioneering forebears, to the breakers of land, the foragers for gold, still acknowledging the contest to achieve nationhood. We are contestants still and we respond beyond most to the sniff of adventure and the hint of challenge.

We are the rugby players we are because a significant ingredient in our make-up expresses our proximity to our early history.

Within the Wellington club we have a very strong Maori influence, much of it injected from the East Coast, we have a strong police membership, we have Salvationists, we have Samoans, Rarotongans, we have surfies, we have lawyers, labourers and lay-preachers.

We have a strong top, men devoted to the club, like Jack Cragg, Bill Brien, Jack Oldershaw. There is a club quality which I believe to be unmatched — though that would buy a fight from Petone, from Ponsonby and Grammar, from Linwood and Belfast, Pirates and Southern and from a whole clutch of clubs, big and small, around the country.

And that is the strength of rugby.

Wellington, character province

It is within the nature of things that the footballer who will never go beyond the club level but who gives his guts and his emotions to his club every week is the forgotten man of rugby. Yet the level of satisfaction they take from a good club performance is no less than that taken by an All Black from a test.

When the Wellington Club went to a champion-of-champions tournament in Auckland in 1980 the atmosphere in the dressing room before the final against Ponsonby was equal to any occasion under Cardiff Arms or Twickenham. This was the test match for a dozen players. It was clear they would play that day far above themselves.

Consider Dun Kaiwai, prison officer, from Ruatoria. A prop. He is more than just "a prop". He is a very powerful tight-head prop, good enough to play provincial rugby in many areas of New Zealand. But in Wellington he is not quite good enough, he knows it and he is dedicated to the club. In my career there have been some memorable All Black occasions. There have been club occasions equally sensational. Many of them have been involved with Dun and others like him who have just played themselves into the ground for their club.

Dun is never going to do anything flashy. He is not going to score a try by laying-on a sidestep to beat the fullback. But it is on him and those like him that the reputations of whizz-kids rise or fall. Even the whizz-kids don't really understand that players like Dun make them whizz-kids. He is irreplaceable in New Zealand rugby.

Dun will tell you he intends being New Zealand's "first black prison superintendent". When I became engaged to Lorraine Downes he asked when I was going to introduce him "to the cook".

There is a bond between us, unspoken but tangible. The night after

Wellington had won the Jubilee Cup in 1985 — after the cancellation of the All Black tour of South Africa — we sat talking and drinking together in the club rooms. A young Maori woman came to us and said with contempt, "You should not be like this. You are chalk and cheese. You are from different worlds." Dun looked long at her. It was sad, he said, that so many people in so many places rejected the possibility of warm relationships between people "of different worlds".

We have a classless sport. We have a sport which influences the lives of many, many more people than those who participate in it as players, coaches or spectators. The country thrives on rugby-funded grounds and amenities. They are everywhere, and for the use of local bodies in what ever way they wish.

After all the controversy of the last few years rugby is on a high in New Zealand. You cannot squeeze a tradition out of a nation. If the administration can appreciate that the rugby tradition regularly needs an enlightened polish-up to ensure it does not become fossilised no sport will overtake it as the sport of the New Zealand masses.

I love all sport. I love to see New Zealand teams playing well to win whether in soccer or rugby league or cricket or netball or hockey or softball or . . . name it. At this time neither league nor soccer has the cross-sectional influence in the country that rugby has. The only sport which could compete with rugby in this is netball.

Rugby projects young New Zealand in the most expressive way: the academics the physical workers, the farmers, the trendies, the new-image boys.

The first player to whom I was introduced when I played for Wellington B was Richard McKenzie . . . "This," I was told, "is the grooviest winger in Wellington." Athletic Park patrons will remember him with his shoulder-length hair flowing behind him as he ran down the grandstand touch. When I met him he was wearing cowboy boots and leather strides.

He was the player for his time. When Mike Clamp came into the Wellington representative team years later I thought it was great for rugby — Mike with his fashion gear and flair — and John Kirwan, another of the new breed, and a trendy like Peter Barlow, the Wellington half-back.

Rugby players cannot be defined in stereotype. The new wave will always roll in with its new expressiveness whether in dress, or style or speech. Within some team limitations your man-in-the-street character is the way you play the game and that is why the administrators of the game must keep pace. If they do not they will never shrug off the players' claim that they are too far removed from the changing face of rugby.

It was inevitable that Ian Upston, Wellington's new selector with a long Petone club affiliation, would opt for Andy Leslie as his captain and number eight in 1977. Perhaps I had had a bonus year in 1976 in Leslie's absence. Though I expected the brakes would go on in 1977 I didn't quite expect they would go on as emphatically as they did.

When the team went off on its northern tour Upston said everyone would have a game. After the Taranaki game, which was lost, it was reasonable for me to expect a game against Waikato. I wasn't being presumptuous but I was jumping out of my jockeys to get a game, to have some sort of opportunity to stake a claim or to show that I had something to offer.

I was not named for Waikato so, clearly, after a full season of representative rugby in 1976 I had not shown him enough to warrant one game on the northern tour. In New Plymouth there had been overtures, if not propositions, to encourage me to change unions. After the selection for the Waikato match I harboured dark thoughts of transfer and there could be no more graphic illustration than that of how deeply I felt about what I saw as a selection-snub.

I felt if it was good enough for the selector to encourage players with the promise that everyone on tour would have a game it was good enough for the players to expect it and to feel pretty edgy when it didn't happen.

My sort of edginess was such that I went to Uppy to ask when I could expect to get a game. He wasn't too impressed with that but nor was I with the rationale . . . "I had to wait for my turn. You will have to wait for yours. Your time will come."

Through the years that followed we developed a fine working and personal relationship. He won my respect in many ways and not the least of them were his honesty and his concern for his players as he went through his nine years as Wellington selector-coach. But that day the young Mexted saw any chance of playing himself into the Wellington team for the match against the Lions slipping remorselessly down the tubes. And, being ambitious as well as highly motivated, that was a kick in what later that same year the French would teach me were "les choses sexuel".

Wellington has been the rugbyman's rugby team for many more years than I can remember. I hope it is always so. I have the strongest impression from reading of the period in which my father played that Wellington was never a team to close a game down, even though the

Ranfurly Shield might have been at stake. In the matches which followed the lifting of the shield from Waikato in 1953 Wellington refused to sit back on points or lock into that defensive system which dictates that the "making" of any shield match is in the hands of the challengers.

That gave me a great kick because I can relate that approach to what I know of Wellington as a player since 1976. There have been periods when for lack of quality in a key position certain limitations have been set but the over-riding philosophy has been that the game is for playing. Within that approach there has been a camaraderie among the players which I doubt is approached by any other province. We enjoy our rugby.

It means that the scenario was set many years ago, probably by guys playing with side-boards and knickerbockers, and has been picked up generation after generation by players and coaches.

One of my crisp memories as a little kid is of an old, old man with wrinkled hands showing me how to pass a rugby ball, how to push the ball with the outside hand and guide it with the inside. Though his hands were gnarled and the voice a little shaky the eyes of that old man were startlingly bright and humorous. He was the father of one of my parents' closest friends. His name was Billy Wallace. From what I have read and heard of his performances for the 1905 team he takes a place high in my list of players I wish, by some sort of mysticism, I could watch playing at their best. I am sure he is one of those pioneers who created the Wellington playing instinct as it is today.

Over the period of the late '70s and early '80s we had the means to indulge that instinct almost endlessly. About the time I took over the captaincy the province lost players like John Heale, half-back, Tu Wyllie, first five-eighths, Dan Fouhy, midfield, Jamie Salmon, centre, Stu Wilson, wing. We did not have the means to move the ball as we wanted and we felt our game becoming stultified.

Ian Upston and I moved urgently to develop a system whereby we consolidated in the forwards, seeking to create positions of advantage for our young and inexperienced backs to gain confidence.

Slowly through 1984 this happened as we planned it so that toward the end of it we had a marvellous game against Auckland at Athletic Park. It had become obvious I would have to do a lot of work from the base of the scrum to either score from forward power or to endeavour to take out a loose forward and a back to give our own backs the space to score.

It was the beginning of a period of my rugby when I became conscious there was some criticism of my "predictability". The criticism did

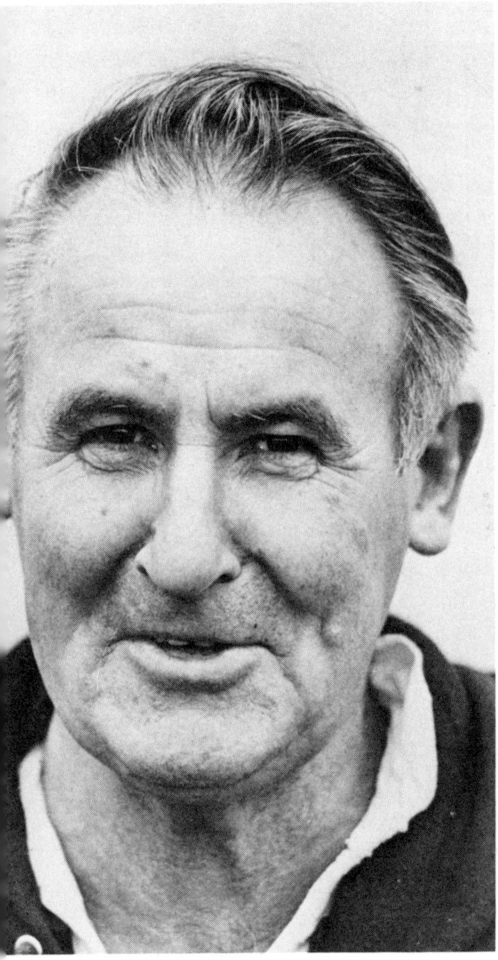

Ian Upston (above), long-serving Wellington coach with whom I developed an excellent understanding after a shaky start. Right: Doing my thing for Wellington.

not bite that year because I scored 18 first-class tries, including seven for the All Blacks in Australia and eight for the province in what was for me a provincial season abbreviated by touring requirements.

The law changes of 1985 forced yet another change with a flanker and number eight able to stand off on one side and a flanker and the half-back on the other. What we had done successfully the previous year now became much more difficult. With the intensified defence patterns the inexperience of some of our back play was exposed. So we planned to use myself as a decoy taking the first couple of strides before feeding one of the flankers who took the plunge so we could set up the ruck. This was marginally successful but as the season progressed there was criticism of my "dogmatic" style of play.

After he had been deposed as Wellington selector-coach for 1986 Ian Upston took me by surprise by going into print on what he saw as my compulsion to use the base of the scrum as my own launching-pad. I was surprised because one of his strengths as a coach was that he allowed the captain to make decisions on the field and throughout the season he had not discussed this aspect with me. Performance of a team is often dictated by the captain's awareness of what is happening on the field and his adjustment to that. I do not feel defensive about how I played and it is true that Wellington went into its final match of the season, against Wairarapa-Bush, having lost only one match. That day we chanced our arm more and our backs, though weakened by the loss of Mike Clamp by foul means, were found wanting.

I will touch on number eight play again and on the "call" system which dictates at All Black level what my action is to be. But for now, writing of Wellington, I would say that the province will continue to express the character and personality in rugby which is distinctively its own. But it must also take strides into the new sophistications of fitness training in specifics. Auckland has already recognised the need for this. Other provinces must keep in touch.

Wellington's successes in recent years have been based on a remarkably powerful scrummaging unit in which the tight-head prop, Scott Crichton, and the loosehead, Brian McGrattan, have formed the strongest crunch-unit in the country. Possession has been another strength with Murray Pierce and Gerard Wilkinson dominating — and never more so than in their encounter with Andy Haden and Gary Whetton at Athletic Park in 1984.

The influence great scrummaging props can have on the game as it is now played in New Zealand below international level has been sharply minimised by law changes designed to pull back injury levels.

Scotty Crichton . . . power-scrummager. *Brian McGrattan . . . the other half.*

Crichton is the upper-level example of my friend Dun Kaiwai — the often unsung hero upon whom New Zealand success rests. In power-scrummaging at the top storey he has no equal. Not even that great servant of New Zealand rugby, Gary Knight, has Crichton power at the scrum. After the Wellington-Scotland match in 1981 Brendan Gard'ner, the Wellington lock, asked the very strong Scottish prop Jim Aitken what he thought of Scotty. Jim shook his head wryly. "I could'na move him, laddie," he said, "I just could'na move him."

There have been various expressions of doubt from national selectors over Scotty's ability to move with the pace of a test match. I once read him described as "the mobile tree-trunk" and that was on the right track, if a little under-stated. He is remarkably quick of reflex, witness his swiftness round the squash court and his 2,1,0,2 defeat of quicksilver Steve Pokere and his 0,0,1,0 annihilation of loose forward Mexted. And in touch-rugby he has amazing agility for one of his bulk.

Two young backs in whom I have faith to go all the way are the centre John Gallagher and half-back Peter Barlow. Gallagher is a strapping Englishman who played his rugby originally from fullback. As a centre, he can make a break, set up his wings and tackle. He has that sharpness and perception which set aside the very good player from the merely good. Barlow came into the Wellington team when the province already had one of the best young half-backs in the country, Neil Sorensen. Barlow explodes from the base of the scrum, ruck or lineout, sets a game alight for loose forwards. His clearance of the ball is still shaded by Sorensen who I judge to be second only to Dave Loveridge in distribution.

I believe the demise of Ian Upston as coach of Wellington was plotted, that he was the victim of an intense campaign of lobbying and that he deserved better, even from an administration he had not always pleased because of his blunt viewpoints. After nine years, during which the province enjoyed substantial success, he did not deserve to be shot down on the first ballot. If the feeling of the administration ran that strongly against him then it must have been known before the meeting which voted him out. I understand there was a tacit agreement between Uppy and senior administrators that when that time came he would be told and he would relinquish the post.

As the new coach, Earle Kirton, gets the feel of the team he will be good for Wellington rugby. Not in the new-broom sense at all but in the natural extroverted appeal he will have to extroverted youngsters. He has a history of quite outstanding coaching feats in England but as an All Black is conscious of the need to build on efficiency in the simple disciplines of the game. He had the insight to call up Graham Williams as his forward aide and that will do wonders for commitment. To me, after my years with Upston, Kirton has something to prove.

To France with love

Early in the 1977 season I had my first New Zealand Trial in one of those matches which are labelled with monumental disregard for for English definition, Possibles versus Probables. It is meant to convey that the players in both teams have equal status, equal chances of carrying on beyond trial selection but I would hope that the difference between "possibility" and "probability" would long since have occurred to the more academic of our national administrators.

I have already referred to the great trial of 1984 and the lesson of team-play it conveyed. The early trial of 1977 was a lesson in reverse. I learned it about ten minutes into the game when Dave Neal, a very good flanker from Marlborough, gathered a loose ball at the back of the lineout and set sail for the line. I ran in close support and as he reached the fullback I called for the pass, unmarked. Dave shaped to pass but pulled the ball back in and tried to beat the fullback, Richard Wilson. He didn't and I'm sure that a pass to me would have impressed the selectors in his favour much more than in mine for the mere formality of the try: trial mentality, that odd malaise which strikes rugby players when they are called Possibles or Probables. Playing for his province Dave Neal would have done the right thing, his mind uncluttered by the jumble of possibilities and probabilities which so often negate the team concept in trials.

In the same match the first time the opposition kicked for goal I positioned myself — as I had always — near the goalposts, to catch the kick and to have the best possible view of the options. One of the experienced All Black midfield backs reprimanded me. It was for a back to catch the ball, he said. I shuffled off sideways somewhere and let a back make a mess of it. A free spirit like John Dougan would have said, "OK. You catch it, skip pass and we'll have them on down the left touch."

I have learned through that sort of experience how important it is to encourage young players to realise they are there as of right, to take the maximum from them and so give them the confidence to express themselves.

After my own trial I watched Lawrie Knight and Gary Seear in the late match and was under no misapprehension that I had a way to go yet. Knight was clearly the number eight for the All Blacks though at 6ft 3 he was at the very minimum I would have considered then to be acceptable for the lineout-jumping number eight. Today he would be too short. Gary Seear, his nearest rival, was 6ft 4½ though, strangely, according to the records, Seear grew half an inch between September and October the following year — 6ft 4½ against the Australians in New Zealand and 6ft 5 on the subsequent tour of the British Isles, an uncommon rate of growth for a 26-year-old! Fluctuating statistics are not unusual. Wellington's Brendan Gard'ner has taken great confidence from seeing his programme height inflated by two inches and his weight by two stone, figures he undoubtedly supplied himself.

At the end of 1977 Seear went on the nine-match tour of Italy and France with Dick Myers of Waikato as his number-eight back-up. Myers played three times at number eight and once on the flank. In 1978 Seear played all three tests against the Australians in New Zealand and then toured Great Britain with Ash McGregor, 6ft 1, as his stand-in. McGregor — through no fault of his — was simply not a number eight for international rugby. He was one of those diligent Southland types who work like beavers but at 6ft 1 there was nowhere for him to go in the set possession phase. Consequently, he played two games at number eight and one on the side of the scrum in a tour of 18 matches. That was an open declaration of failure by the selection panel, Jack Gleeson, Eric Watson and Peter Burke.

Though I may be seen to be in a position of self-interest in this — because I was deeply disappointed not to make that tour — I could not believe that such a basic blunder would be perpetrated. It was unfair to McGregor, who sat out the tour in increasing intervals — three matches, then five, then the last eight. Jack Gleeson was forced to convert the lock John Fleming to number eight. He played conscientiously and well while the specialist fretted through the matches from the grandstand.

As I contemplate my adversaries through the years I know that my successor as the New Zealand number eight has to be 6ft 4 at the very

My first New Zealand trial and a foot out to impede Dave Loveridge en route to Lyn Davis

Running in support of John Spiers as activities hot up from number 11.

least. We do not want a number eight who is a good player everywhere else, but merely adequate in the lineout. Natural spring can achieve only so much; I have survived because of my absolute desperation against people like Theuns Stofberg, 6ft 6, Jean-Luc Joinel, 6ft 5, Ernesto Ure, Argentina, 6ft 7.

All countries have awoken to the need for players of height for that number seven position in the lineout. Australia has had fine foraging forwards like Ross Reynolds and Peter Lucas but when the chips were down neither could compete adequately at the lineout. That is why the Wallabies brought through so quickly the young New South Welshman Steve Tuynman, 6ft 5. The disadvantage of having a non-competitive player jumping at seven became distressingly clear to the Australians as it has to others. In international rugby you are dicing with disaster if you give the opposition a free ride in a key possession phase.

At the end of the 1977 season I had my first tour abroad with the Wellington Club. It was a threshhold tour for me because at the end of it I passed through the portals to France and in that one act my perception of rugby broadened and my love for it deepened.

My club has a distinguished record in its attention to young players — tours abroad every few years, constant concern that players should participate in every facet of club life. The 1977 tour was for the senior A team and it covered matches in the United States, the United Kingdom, Holland and the East.

The first match was against Orange County, California, and we went into it with forwards like Ted Cox at 6ft 5½, Brendan Gard'ner, 6ft 4½, Gary Senior, 6ft 4½, Paul William, 6ft 3½ and myself, 6ft 4. A big, big pack by any standards, we thought. After the game, which we won comfortably, one of the Americans said, "You guys are small, but my God you're tough." They were gigantic. No sense of patterned rugby or of basic drills, but they galumphed after the play with ten-league boots, formed an elephantine scrum and allowed us to stand in their shadows at the lineouts.

The Americans will play in the first World Cup and that is a bold move with an eye to the future of the game internationally. The invitation to play in a sport with a great world festival has been thrown out and accepted. Should it entice the Americans to turn more than their gridiron rejects toward rugby, should it bolster the game in the colleges — however long it may take — it will eventually bring towering new excitement to international rugby.

I had written to a few French clubs, on the advice of a friend, and

My first day in Agen, 1977. A visit from Stu Wilson and Graham Mourie on tour with the All Blacks. Shortly afterwards Mourie talked to me about number eight play and that was the beginning.

the first response came from Agen. It was encouraging in a non-committal sort of way — come on over, we're interested. It fitted in with the end of the European segment of the club tour so, along with the Agen Club, I shrugged and said, why not?

My French connection had started nearly a decade before, a light love affair rather than a heavy scene; no bedroom consummation, just a vision of the beauty of French rugby from the distance between the middle of Athletic Park and the embankment by the Millard Stand. It was not even French rugby at its best, that test at Athletic Park in 1968, but there were such glimpses of its intent, such tantalising moments of Maso that I was intrigued, and when Villepreux kicked that prodigious goal from far into his own half it was as much an expression of French impracticality as it was anything else. He had no right to kick the goal. It was impractical that he should even consider it. So, being French, he kicked it.

The French have a history of big lineout sevens — Joinel, Erbani, Carpentier, Bastiat, Esteve, Claude and Walter Spanghero, Dauga. They love to throw the ball deep so they have this imposing list of slab-bodied athletes jumping there. So it is not just the height of the player at seven;

it is his physical presence. The French love a big forward — provided he is a **good** big forward. They are quick to turn on the big man who lacks athleticism. That day at Athletic Park it was Walter Spanghero while Dauga, locking the scrum, was in the middle of the line.

Locking with Dauga was Alain Plantefol, the man who so dispassionately booted Colin Meads in the head at Colombes the year before and who, when I arrived at Agen nine years later, was still playing and a bulwark of the club.

There was always with me, so long before I went to Agen, an excitement about French rugby. It was something of the fluency and rhythm I would relate to black men playing the game — though that probably will put me on someone's black list. In sporting terms I can think of no greater compliment than to suggest a player or competitor has the rhythm which seems to come naturally to the black, for without rhythm and timing all the grafting platform-work of, say, the New Zealand forwards would go for nothing. That's what the French have.

So I anticipated Agen with excitement. I knew no French, I knew nothing of their customs, I knew "oui" and "non". I was asked where in France I was going. "To Agen."

"Ah, yes, but where in Agen."

"I dunno. Rue something."

That is how prepared I was.

When I arrived I was met by a great man of Agen rugby, Pierre Lacroix. I knew of him. He had toured New Zealand with the 1961 French team, a square-built and courageous half-back. Pierre confronted the big media presence as my interpreter though his English seemed to just about parallel my French. Yet every three-word answer I gave to questions Pierre translated into 100 of French.

The next morning I commanded an impressive spread in the papers. My god, what was this? The great All Black? The fastest loose forward in New Zealand? The scorer of a thousand tries and the kicker of 500 goals? Sought by every club in France but won by Agen through brilliant negotiation?

Somewhere in the stories there were elements of truth, I'm sure. But as to the colossal exaggerations no one cared. Pierre didn't care, the people of Agen didn't care. It was all great publicity for the club, the build-up to bring hundreds and hundreds more people through the turnstiles. So what is a little embarrassment, Murree? All New Zealanders are All Blacks to us. Come, Murree, a glass of wine. We will drink to rugby. And so we did. Often.

The first week of Agen was a week of adventure. Everything new,

Completely at home in the Cafe La Poste, Agen, with French internationals Daniel Dubroca, left, and Christian Beguerie, right, and fellow Wellingtonian Geoff Campbell.

When in France . . . dinner following Agen training . . . wine in the soup and the traditional slurp.

everything exotic. It was like a kid opening up a Christmas stocking, a surprise in every package. But from there things went sour. My inability to communicate on the simplest things, the need I felt to say what I felt about rugby; the French newspapers were French, the French radio was French, the French magazines were French. They put a mark at the top of their figure 1 so that I mistook it for a seven, they made jokes and laughed in French, they talked tactics in French, they looked puzzled in French when I asked for a pint of milk.

And then, the unkindest cut of all, the last straw . . . They tried to teach me how to jump in the lineout in French. We hadn't been getting much ball and this old guy, uncoordinated as he was, started to give me kindergarten lessons in how to jump. Everything collided in my mind. A frustration-haemorrhage. To hell with this, I said, and stormed off, with dramatic gestures in the international language. No mistakes here. Perfect understanding . . . I'm off home where people speak English, where a figure 1 is a figure 1, where jokes are jokes and I don't have to say "moo" when I want a bottle of milk.

As I walked away they called after me, "Murree, Murree, ou tu va, ou tu va?" I brushed past Nelson, the stadium custodian, poor guy, not his fault with his beret over one eye while the other looked worried. I was undoing my boots when I was aware of someone standing there. I started to say "What the hell . . ." when I saw Nelson was offering me a towel and soap and looking like a cuffed pup.

Showered and fuming still, I stormed away from the ground to my apartment. I asked myself half a dozen questions and each time came up with the same answer: go home. I was packing when Rene Benesis knocked at the door. Rene was a hooker in the most manly sense of the word. He carried the most beautifully descriptive title in all of rugby: le talonneur. Rene, in fact, was le talonneur magnifique, a veteran of 30 matches for France when he was playing out of Narbonne in the '60s and early '70s.

In fractured English Rene asked me to hear his story. Over a glass of wine and an atlas he explained he came to Agen from a tiny village outside Narbonne. As was accepted, he was lured to Agen with a house, a job, money, the "prime" for the match won.

Coming from a hamlet to Agen, population about 37,000, he felt lost and alone . . . "And French is my language. But you? Nouvelle-Zelande. No language. No customs. How must **you** feel? What is your emotion?" And Rene told me he had been watching me, understanding what I was going through but feeling unable to help.

"Come, Murree. We will go to the cafe." And we did and we talked

Never let the ball die: the French attitude.

and Rene persuaded me to stay for two more weeks, to give Agen that chance. Within two weeks I met Joelle, a lady of Limoges. She took me out of suffocation and into the champagne life of France. Joelle had been junior sprint champion of France and was now a physical education teacher. The better we came to know each other and the more we shared the nightlife of Limoges or skied at Val D'Isere the less convivial became my relationship with her former boyfriend, a flanker in the Agen B team. Every week when the A team trained with the B team, he would be having a crack at me while I was dazed in anticipation of another night in Limoges. At the end of it all there was no animosity. When I left he gave me six bottles of Pomerol '62 and I gave him my footy socks, which seemed a fair exchange to me.

My infatuation with Joelle was essentially an infatuation with France — an affair with France, if you like. It brought me into the sort of life of which I had dreamed when I first considered playing in France and it blew away my confused frustration over life in Agen and with Agen. It restored vitality to my everyday existence and with that my rugby prospered. I was drawn into the family-life of Pierre Lacroix and his wife, Nicole, and of Jean and Nicole Holt from whom I learned a broad range of idiomatic French — so much so that I could be understood, I could understand, I could converse.

Pierre loves rugby more than any man I know. He weeps for the love of rugby. When he reminisces on his tour with the 1961 team, the tears well and overflow. When he talks of the try Kel Tremain scored in the insane storm at Athletic Park he weeps because it was he who passed the ball to Claude Lacaze over the French line before Lacaze kicked it into the charging Tremain. But he weeps, too, for the try scored into the tempest by his own winger Jean Dupuy.

To play club rugby in France you must understand the significance of playing at home and playing away. Playing at home you go down on the ball and everything is OK. Playing away you never go down on the ball unless you have it in you to die for your club. In other words, in home matches you kick the hell out of them and in away games they kick the hell out of you.

The average French club is not expected to win away. If you do it's a fantastic achievement — and the "prime" (the bonus) is too big to be stuffed in the toe of your boot.

French referees apply great favouritism to the home side for a number of reasons: the home side expects to win at home; the visiting team expects to lose; the home crowd is so aggressively partisan that it is in the interests of self-preservation that the referee steers his favours toward the home team.

My first away game was at Auch. Playing from the side of the scrum I scored a try after about 20 minutes. At the following scrum my opponent stood up and kicked me squarely on the nose. He had no fear of reprimand from a referee sensitive more for his own skin than my nose, now of a shape rarely seen outside a skid-row boxing gym. The doctor advised me to leave the field, a kindly offer which I refused. I did not contemplate reprisal at that stage but as the game got under way and I noted the self-satisfied look on the kicker's face I decided he had to be sorted out.

At a lineout the ball was in the air as I turned to investigate the comparative resilience of the Gallic nez to the Anglo-Saxon nose. But he fled at the speed of sound. I chased him and he sprinted over the sideline, leaped the fence, and lost himself among the crowd in the grandstand. Coming back on? Non. Definitely non. He was replaced. As I scored a second try he was up there somewhere among the spectators making intelligent conversation about the game.

We won and that was a matter for great jubilation — as far as one can express jubilation with his nose against his cheekbone. At home

Performing for Agen, 1980, on the ground to which the French had me betrothed, Armandie.

the way to overcome that sort of discomfort is to take a beer or so. The other players were into wine but I ordered my beer and another and another by which time Christian Vivies, one of our players, judged I needed company. Four days later he delivered me back to Agen in time for training. He spoke no English and I knew a few lines of Frere Jacques. So we sang it. Many, many times. I forgot my nose. I learned to talk with my eyes, my hands.

Christian introduced me to fine company in all the cafes and nightclubs of Auch and beyond. When the cafes closed at 2 a.m. he took me to nightclubs, sometimes 50 kilometres distant. France was starting to feel like home.

The French have a profound sense of symmetry. The following game, some player, distressed at the lack of symmetry in my nose, punched it straight.

After an away game against Tyrosse which we won narrowly the referee surrendered himself to us at the last whistle. We fought our way through the indignant fans and he was taken away in a security wagon. After another in the east of France I went to thank the referee. He took a swift look at me as I approached him purposefully, took to his scrapers, bolted into the toilet and slammed the door. I stood there feeling like some sort of voyeur, shouting, "Monsieur, Monsieur, merci for the match." He misunderstood my intentions. He did not emerge.

In the earliest days, when things were difficult, there was a common language — the rugby language. When I was there to take a pass I said "oui" instead of "ball" and "j'ai" instead of "my ball" when I was under the kick. There was no selfishness. As the caller I had right of way, whether taking the kick or the pass. Where in New Zealand everyone would be fighting for the pass and creating difficulties, there was acceptance and one of the lessons I learned from French rugby was that you did not call unless it was exactly right for you because on the call you got your pass.

The French style is to create play for the man most advantageously placed to do something with it. They get as much pleasure from putting someone else into a gap as in slicing through themselves. Where in New Zealand we tend to try to make holes, the French create holes. Every Frenchman is a Bruce Robertson in his attention to creating the best situation of advance for his team. Graham Mourie, who played a lot of rugby in France, has this same mentality: the gap is for the most effective runner.

There are reasons for all this. The French rugby player has great breadth of vision. He sees or senses what is going on around him. If he is in any doubt that he can get through a gap he will make the decision at the split-second ultimate to let someone else do it, that inevitable Frenchman running in support from depth.

The Frenchman hates to be castled ball and all — that's not within his concept of rugby. He wants to keep the ball alive, the rhythm beating. Often in New Zealand rugby — and I am part of it — we put our heads down, charge, set up the ruck. That's not the French style.

In recent years my own style has become more stereotyped because of the influence on it of South African rugby. I am conscious of it and I believe that had I continued to play in France my game would have been much more expansive. If I have any regret about the way my rugby has developed it is that perhaps it has lost some of that French breadth of vision, some of the freedom of expression.

I doubt whether any other country has had the supreme experience of seeing French rugby as New Zealanders saw it in 1984. I speak specifically of their performance against Wellington. To me, knowing them, it was the total expression of everything I have loved in their rugby.

I had no great affection for it that day. Captaining Wellington and in the middle of a great forward effort from my players I watched events in the last quarter of that match with a desperate sort of need to stop the French from flying, yet with a feeling born from intimate knowledge of them that they were flying so high it would take an act of God to put the brakes on them. In the last 15 minutes they scored four tries of magical beauty to beat Wellington 38-18 — and this after Wellington had fought back from 0-15 to 15-18, seeming to have the French ready for the sword. Then Lescarboura and Lagisquet, Codorniu, Esteve and Blanco uncorked the bubbly.

Those who were there and those who watched it on television should treasure that exhibition. They may never see its like again.

Every player has an acute appreciation of tactics when he has the ball in hand and when he is running in support. French backs run on different angles from us to straighten up play. They see little of merit in our endeavours to breach advantage close to the forwards. They are running on from depth wide out to create the break. It is as much in them as body-positioning at the ruck is in us — it is intuitive.

At the end of my French experience in 1980 there was evidence I had given something to Agen and that Agen had given much to me. Agen gave me far greater self-assurance on the field, the confidence and the opportunity to do things which rarely arise in New Zealand. yet had I not the New Zealand grounding I could not have assimilated these things as quickly as I did. The New Zealand efficiency was a sturdy baseplate from which to grasp other opportunities.

They told me I had brought them new hope in what had threatened to be a bad year for them in 1977-78; that there was a resurgence of the previous year's buoyancy where there might have been a financial slump . . . "Many, many people came to see you, came to judge this New Zealander, came to condemn or to be convinced that the club had done the right thing. They came back and back because you gave them your own gift of excitement," Pierre Lacroix said. "You gave our children, our players of the future, your time and your friendship. That is without price . . ."

Pierre, you understand, has a great gift for overstatement. I can measure only what Agen especially and what all of French rugby did for me.

But talking of Agen's finances, let me lay my cards face-up. In 1977 I went into a job driving a cheese-truck. Monsieur Clerc, my boss, paid me what other cheese-truck drivers received. And fine cheeses they were. But my accommodation was paid, my car and petrol were provided and so were several meals every week. So, my net earnings were truly net. There could have been more. But I told them I didn't want their money. I was there to play rugby. Once, when things were going specially well for the club, a member took me aside and said there would be a fine bonus. Not necessary, I said.

As the season progressed I was required to work less by M. Clerc. There was a need, it seemed, to save my energy for the match. "You must not work so hard," said the club. "You must take more time off." I told them I couldn't afford to take days off. "Oh, but yes you can," said the club. "Do not worry. Your pay will be the same, will it not, M. Clerc?" And M. Clerc beamed and nodded. Vive Agen. Vive les fromages Francais.

Reflection is a worthwhile pastime. On reflection I realised much more about my presence in Agen. The club created so much publicity about their "All Black" and his unworldly gifts that for the first game I played there were 2500 more spectators than normally they would have expected. It was the first time any of the strong clubs had imported a foreign player and it was seen to be a matter of almost erotic moment.

They marketed me as we might market butter — but with considerably more flair. It was important, they told me, that I play well. Of course it was important. The 2500 extra spectators were bringing in $NZ25,000 more per match. With a minimum of ten home games I work out, by counting on fingers and toes, that the increased gate revenue is $NZ250,000. From a home match the host team takes 60 per cent of the gate, the visiting team 20 per cent and the French Rugby Federation 20 per cent and that all seems to add up to an extra $NZ150,000 income a season for Agen.

Fortunately my first game was a good one. I scored two tries. The administrators were happy. The players were happy. The spectators were happy. The referee was happy because the home team had won and he was safe for another day.

The significance of all this did not strike me till the following year when Agen pleaded for my return. Non, I said, I cannot. And each time I said non Agen said oui and talked in franc-type telephone numbers . . . my job, of course, was there. Everyone was very self-righteous about that. The need to preserve one's amateur status is devoutly recognised in France. Everyone knows that. But because I was such a good and conscientious cheese-truck driver in 1977 M. Clerc would see fit to pay me much more next time. Like double, Murree? Like treble, Murree? Like what is it you want, Murree?

The assumption was that I was holding out. In fact, I did not want to go back the following season. I could have asked for $NZ2000 a

The deal is clinched. Less work more money. Agen, 1980.

month and it would have been chicken-feed compared with the gate increase if the team was winning and I was playing well. So, by accident, I discovered just what I was worth to them.

I discovered, too, how much I was worth to Limoges. The president of Limoges was Coco Peron who ran a nightclub I had frequented with Joelle and who had a finger in various other mischievous operations. To be president of a French club is highly prestigious. To get there Coco, for instance, had to be very generous, a provider. Not to put too fine a point on it, the guy who puts most money into the club becomes president.

Having observed with bulging eyes what a foreign player could do for Agen, Coco considered it an entirely reasonable thing that the same player should do the same thing for Limoges the following year. I turned him down, too. But there was much food for reflection in all this. I arranged for Al Keown to go to Limoges and for Geoff Campbell, a finely-built Wellington player who seemed to have a big future, to go to Agen. The day he arrived at Agen he shared the front page of Sud-Ouest with Mitterand. "The New Mexted; Agen's Second All Black" proclaimed Sud-Ouest. The Agen propaganda machine was well oiled.

When I went to Agen, ostensibly to visit, after the All Black tour of England and Scotland in 1979, I found a sort of folk-hero environment. They had seen live on television the try I scored against Scotland and the Agen boys hooked into that for all they were worth . . . "This is what Agen created," they said. "Without his season in Agen he could not have achieved this." And the people of Agen were eager to believe it. And, who knows, there might have been shades of truth in it.

I would play for them now, in 1979? No, I must go home. If I stayed it could be only till February; it would upset the team pattern. Only till February? OK. We accept. And I could see the big-franc signs light up in their eyes. I aimed at the moon. "For $NZ8000?" No hesitation. Oui. Oui, oui, oui. "Just to cover my expenses, you understand." But, of course, Murree, there are many expenses.

M. Clerc's cheese-trucks bounded about the countryside without my help. I had lots of skiing. I played well for Agen and I played well for myself off the field. Geoff Campbell came on to his game strongly and Agen was specially delighted about that.

New Zealand players contemplating rugby in France must not make the mistake of going into it as a continental holiday. The French are great if their import is playing well. Everyone supports you, there is a contest to entertain you. But if the team is not playing well there is a strong tendency to regard the foreign player as the culprit. He is ignored, even ostracised, and his life becomes unpleasant.

Brendan Gard'ner played for a middle-of-the-road club in a rugby league town, Carcassonne, an hour and a half by train from Agen. Brendan — or Compost as we call him in Wellington — fitted the French hero-image superbly. A big man, Compost, and the French revere big men. The pressure went on him when Carcassonne was in danger of relegation. The club turned on him and virtually placed the saving of their status in his hands; his responsibility as a New Zealand rugby player.

During my first season with Agen I visited Compost at Carcassonne, a social visit. Carcassonne had just played Claude Spanghero's Narbonne team and about 2.30 a.m. we joined Claude for a drink in a nightclub. Big Claude was a dominating figure, not by means of his size alone, but for his presence and his popularity. To Compost and me there seemed to be a hell of a lot of fine champagne meandering around the club without much purpose. So we gave it some purpose. Every time a waiter with a tray came within striking distance — and between us we had an impressive length of arm — we struck.

We knew it was all part of the hospitality and considered it would be boorish not to show appreciation. We were rather taken aback by the "little glasses", though. In fact, they were elegant champagne flutes but to a couple of jug-and-flagon jokers from over the sea they were "little glasses" and they didn't seem to hold a satisfying volume of champagne. Logically, then, we opined, we must take volume from frequency.

Between seasons . . . my brother Alan and I at Sunset Beach, Hawaii, Alan returning to Wellington, I on route to Europe and South Africa, while Dad holds Mexted Motors together.

It's hell in Africa. On the Okavango Swamps, Botswana, one week before the All Black trial 1983.

My first rugby tour, 1977, with the Wellington Football Club. At the Heineken Brewery, Amsterdam . . . Kelvin Tait, Tom Bracefield, Charlie Henderson and Brendan Gard'ner.

The reason St Francis Bay has become renowned throughout the surfing world. The insigificant black blur is me.

Wellington-Otago, a challenge on the promising Otago halfback Dean Kenny.

The immediate despondency of a lost test match — Wellington, 1982, second test against Australia.

Claude Spanghero was highly amused by all this. every time we waylaid another waiter Claude laughed. The waiters looked first nonplussed then, seeing Claude laughing, laughed in a distracted sort of way with him, before diving away. Claude, and progressively more and more of the guests, were so entertained by it all that we thought it a reasonable thing to give them their money's worth and the waiters were so magnetised by his amusement that they kept coming within arms-length. So we drank champagne out of "little glasses" for more than an hour and laughed along with Claude.

The next day the whole town was laughing. The champagne belonged to a wedding party in an ante-room and the waiters were desperately trying to keep pace with demand at the top table. Claude knew it. We didn't.

Male chauvinism is a thriving animal in rugby-playing France. Every child in the womb is a potential rugby player . . . "You have had a baby? Well done. Boy or girl? A girl? Oh, hard luck. Better luck next time."

What is it, then, which drives the French to such provocative lengths to ensure that teams touring their country have as much inconvenience and frustration as possible? In spite of the hassles of 1981 and, I believe, 1977, New Zealand players react to that sort of organised chaos in just the way the French would prefer they did not. It is a romantic dream to propose this essentially French activity draws a team closer together. With New Zealanders the task-in-hand is paramount. All Blacks may experience transient anger but are hard-headed about the essentials of touring — winning the tests.

The French intentionally appoint a nincompoop as a liaison officer with a touring team. And when the touring team tires of his ineptitude and demands a replacement they replace him with an idiot. This is what happened in 1981. The original liaison officer — almost a professional in the field — created so much havoc that he was seen to be a highly successful laison officer by the French. When it became clear to him that everyone was awake to the scheme he resigned. So the French Federation appointed a man I knew from my Agen days — a notorious idiot. Perfect for the job. He didn't even have to act the part.

Our manager, Pat Gill, was inclined to take everything at face value — certainly out of concern for the players — and we had panic stations while the French, with all their blandness and apparent deep concern, were mentally falling all over the place laughing.

The problems of management on that tour were alleviated by the presence of Richard Palmer, formally interpreter, but actually liaison officer and negotiator — a New Zealander who had lived in France for six years. And perhaps even more significantly Andrew Maxwell Haden was a commanding presence, respected by the French Rugby Federation president, Albert Ferrasse. It was a mutual respect/affection thing with Andy knowing what Ferrasse was all about and Ferrasse knowing Andy knew.

If New Zealanders who take satisfaction from putting Haden down for his commercialism and his self-projection, could overcome their prejudice they might at the very least start to appreciate what he has done for rugby and its players and what he is continuing to do. The old traditionalists of rugby, before judging Haden, should always consider that his activities within the game have been unselfish, that he sought and won understanding of the players' plight in a modern world where jobs no longer grow on goalposts, where families cannot subsist on the generosity of employers and where pride in the silver fern — as strong as ever — can no longer counter-balance the practicalities of life.

In France he can banter with the French in their own tongue, understand their subtleties, their perverseness, their sense of humour. They love it. They love an Anglo-Saxon bon-vivant who speaks the language fluently. They are contemptuous of the Anglo-Saxon who trudges heavily through their country without effort to pick up at least a smattering of the tongue.

Haden's sheer size creates the environment — it is that big-is-beautiful syndrome again. But it is also that he carries his size with unconscious ease rather than walking into a room and endeavouring to fill it with size and sound as many big men do. He doesn't strut his 6ft 7; he walks it as if it's 5ft 9.

Brash entrepreneur? There's natural humility in the man. Not in the same way as Colin Meads or Brian Lochore is humble, because Haden is a projector, a voluble enthusiast, a publicist, an innovator, a humourist. Yet if you have any gift of insight at all you quickly reach into his humility and pride.

Albert Ferrasse is seen in New Zealand as some sort of bull-mastiff, getting his teeth into our pants, worrying away at us with infuriating persistence. Certainly the bull-mastiff is there in the same way as it was there in Churchill — and is in Danie Craven. But this monstre terrible has charisma, class and command. He is quick to condemn touring managers in whom he detects naivety or weakness.

They call him Monsieur President not Monsieur Ferrasse. A man of Agen, he once asked me what I thought of the club. I said, "Tout est possible avec l'equipe d'Agen." Later the club produced a history.

My Agen experience follows me home. Pierre Lacroix at Bill Brien's pub in Wellington.

In the preface Ferrasse quoted this as a tribute to Agen by a player from a country where rugby is a religion.

Ferrasse is ruthless. His smiles are often on the face of the tiger. He moves aggressively to put right what he sees are the actions of fools. In 1979 when I was in France I was told there were actually 13 French selectors, one for each position but two for props (tighthead and loose). So moved are selectors, whether at club or international level, by the win-loss situation that these selectors by individual choice changed nearly every player after a poor Five Nations performance.

Among those to go were the scrum-half, Jerome Gallion, and the fly-half, Alain Caussade. Their replacements were interviewed at length on radio and television, their pictures with interviews were in the newspapers. They said all those things you might expect. They were "greatly honoured" to play for their country. They felt "very humble". They would lay down their lives, if necessary, for France.

They were never placed in that dire predicament. The following morning Ferrasse announced with enigmatic dignity that there had been a reappraisal and all the players from the previous game were reselected. He did not add "by me". He did not need to.

Ferrasse judged that I gave my guts every time I played for Agen. He never forgot. When I went back to France in 1984 to sell scrummaging machines I needed him. I knew that if I could sell one of the machines to a top club others would follow. So, I called on Ferrasse. He engineered a selling environment very simply. He called in five of the club's top administrators, gave each of them ten names of influential club members and said, "Go. Convince them to buy." They did.

I suppose that further cemented my affection for Agen — not that I needed mercenary gain to do that. Agen and its people are a part of my life — they sharpened my taste for life and then showed me how to savour it. In Agen they called me "le fiance d'Armandie". Armandie is the Agen ground and, in that context, its supporters. My betrothal to Armandie was a love-match. It was an honour to me that the feeling was mutual.

The influence of the French experience on my rugby and, I suppose, on my developing personality, may be gauged by my automatic reaching for French players when I am asked to talk of the impact of overseas players on my career.

I think immediately of Claude Spanghero, of Jean-Pierre Rives, of Jean-Luc Joinel and of a host of others who though of lesser stature than those three, maybe no more than club players, have played their part in the education of Mexted.

Roger Uttley . . . a lesson in tolerance.

But even having gone so instinctively to the French players I always check myself and recall an early lesson in composure and tolerance from an English player for whom I developed great admiration: Roger Uttley of Gosforth, North of England. He played something over 20 times for England and was part of the great British Isles triumph in South Africa in 1974. There the Lions converted Uttley from a second row forward to a flanker and gave him a vital jumping role at the back of the lineout. Now it was 1979 and North were giving us a hiding, beating us to the loose ball with Uttley, Peter Dixon and Tony Neary. Frustrating stuff for a young number eight on his first All Black tour, so much so that at one lineout I was sufficiently ill-advised to reach up and take a swing at Uttley. This tall, gangling man with the hatchet face and the jagged mouth looked down at me without rancour, almost sorrowfully, and said, "Settle down, sunshine." It was the kindly headmaster taking pity on the recalcitrant schoolboy but saying unmistakeably, "Do it again and I'll cane you. In the meantime, let's forget it."

And then I come back to France and Claude Spanghero and my first lesson in short lineouts. Agen v Narbonne. Claude, 6ft 7, an enormous man but skilled and athletic. Narbonne pulled the two-man lineout. I was on Claude. He faked forward, then back, . . . I never knew which way he was going. I learned to combat him as best I could by standing in such a manner that I forced him to go one way. Predictable, but with a man like him still a mountainous task to contest the ball. Claude to me typifies the rugged French loose forward who in most countries would be seen as a lock — and a big, strong lock at that.

And Jean-Luc, my favourite opponent and my hardest. Jean-Luc has it all, equally effective as flanker and number eight, but always the number seven lineout jumper and for many seasons France's main source of lineout possession. Again we find this agility the French take for granted in their big men, but in Jean-Luc it is extraordinary even for the French. Of all the players I have marked he has been the ultimate personal challenge. I knew I had to be at maximum alertness, utterly reactive to match him. To beat him was a rare personal triumph, a transient event over in seconds to come my way hopefully again some time. I met him first when he played for Brive and then a year later when Wellington played the French touring team of 1979. Since those days we have been at each other's throats — metaphorically, of course — and it is the greatest tribute I can imagine that he sees me as a worthy competitor.

He has become, in his own way, almost as much of a cult figure as Jean-Pierre Rives. His club crowd and, when he plays internationals, his French crowd chant with massive rhythm, "Jean-Luc, Jean-Luc, Jean-Luc." In the second test in 1981 at Parc des Princes in which the French used Jean-Luc incessantly at the lineout the pair of us were involved in an intense man-on-man struggle. After it, we regarded each other with the warmest respect and after a few drinks we agreed solemnly that he was the best and I was the best.

Jean-Pierre epitomises everything the French love in a sportsman. He fits the bill perfectly, tailor-made to appeal to the media and to Latin romanticism. He had to be le capitaine, born to be the leader, the flowing blond hair, the blood-stained white jersey, the gay bachelor, the darling of society, pursued by long-legged beauties from all over the world, a prize to be won if only fleetingly. Yes and a rugby player, too, as committed to his team and his fans on the field as he was to his exotic lifestyle off it. The French Mourie on the field. But no Mourie off it. But it was he who sparked a series of events through which I discovered Mourie could really relax.

In 1982 Mourie, Gary Knight and I were invited to play for the British Barbarians first in a warm-up game at Waterloo and then against a French XV to mark the centennial celebrations of the Racing Club of Paris. When we checked in to our Paris hotel Jean-Pierre was drift-

Claude Spanghero . . . master of the fake.

ing languidly through the foyer, his long white scarf wrapped about his neck, clothed like a model for casual fashionwear. It is a measure of the man's intelligence that when I asked him if he had something organised after the game he knew exactly what I had in mind. He smiled. "I will be having a big party. It will be good and you will be there." And he wrote an address and gave it to me.

Disorganisation bordering on chaos is what the French after-match dinner may appear to be to the uninformed outsider. Actually it is simply that flexibility is the key. In my own case I found some old friends from Agen and in a slight haze went with them to a bar of which my memory is slightly foggy other than that there was a great deal of good red wine and many old guys wearing berets. Suddenly it was 12.30 am. I said we must leave immediately and go to Jean-Pierre's party. Soon, soon, they said. Soon, soon, they kept saying and I knew daylight would beat me to the party. So I left. But I had no idea where I was. It was raining. It was all very strange. So I hailed a taxi, told the driver the party-venue and he took off as only French taxi-drivers know how. Some time later he took his foot off the accelerator and put it on the brake for the first time. This was it, he said. I'm sure it was. Nightclubs everywhere. Very fashionable. Very trendy. "C'est impossible," I said. And I said it again to someone I'd never seen before. And I explained the impossibility of finding the private party of Jean-Pierre Rives in this thousand-party circus. But non. The name Jean-Pierre worked the oracle. Everyone knew where Jean-Pierre was throwing his party.

The doorman at the big nightclub looked at me forbiddingly. He was built like a chateau and he had this terrible facial disfiguration caused, I immediately assumed, by performing heroic deeds in a back alley. When I said "Jean-Pierre" the face softened from granite to rock and he showed me through.

The place was populated by beautiful women, 80 of them by a slightly stupefied count, and every one a knock-out. To my left a fountain bubbled pure champagne, a Dixie-style band played and here and there were chaps in blazers. It was Jean-Pierre at his best. Here was the chic beauty-world that was Paris. I thought if I moved too quickly or talked loudly it would all disappear in a puff of pink smoke. I said something quietly in French to a young lady. She answered in perfect American. She told me most of the girls were not French but were high quality models from all over the world, part of the agency Delphine. Someone interrupted to talk about rugby and I thought that was pretty damned inconsiderate and when I turned back she had taken off her big picture hat. I mentioned this and found she was actually a different girl.

The two girls and I went off nightclubbing, which brought happiness to my heart and cardiac arrest to my credit card. We arranged to have dinner the next night and, with great reluctance, parted. I invited Mourie to dinner and from that meeting he shed the cloak of aloofness and the rigid decorum of the touring captain I had known. We tasted fine wines far into the night and we invited the ladies to join us for a joyful but impeccably virtuous weekend at The Cock, a picturesque pub over the channel in Hatfield Broadoak. Our host would be Mr Dave Durrell, spoofer — in fact, entertainment co-ordinator for all spoofers.

Hatfield Broadoak, population about 100 foxhunters, welcomed us with all its olde-world hospitality. Two All Blacks, two beautiful models and open-night at The Cock — a great occasion for the village. Mr Durrell didn't close the pub that night. The fire blazed, the songs were sung, the fine ale flooded down willing throats.

For the first time in my experience of him I watched Graham Mourie really relax. I had the feeling he was in an element he yearned for, that this was the sort of relaxation he would never allow himself as captain of New Zealand. He was amusing, charming and generous, — somehow, I felt, the **real** Mourie, the one not many of his friends and certainly very few of his fellow players ever saw.

At 3 am there was an ominous beating on the door of the pub. Me: Who is it? Voice: It's the police. Me: Oh, sure, ha-ha. And I opened the door. It was the police.

He pointed at Mr Durrell. "Got you," he said. "This time, Durell, I've got you." Mr Durrell said. "Good evening officer. Have you met Graham Mourie, All Black captain, and Murray Mexted, All Black number eight?" It was a master stroke.

The constable had not met us but plainly was overwhelmed to do so. And when Mr Durrell said, "And could I possibly interest you in a pint, officer?" and the girls moved in one to each of his arms, the law was lost. One of the girls had his helmet on, he gave his tunic buttons to the other, then he went home, put on the local rugger club pullover, came back and said he was not remotely interested in leaving for a very long time.

Hatfield Broadoak is far from the habitat of Jean-Pierre Rives but I digress without apology because for me, to have Mourie as company in this sort of environment, was a true experience.

Jean-Pierre the rugby player was one of deep character and courage. He specialised in making the ball available, in attaining possession and retaining possession.

Formidable, Jean-Pierre, formidable.

The first fern

Thank god for half-time. A suck on an orange, a rub on the knee, an agonising reappraisal, coach and captain pouring words, redirecting strategy, goading individuals, hoarse breathing . . . Graham Mourie and Peter Burke are looking at me. They're saying we've been getting no ball in the lineout at middle and front, we're in trouble at 10-4 down to a confident South Island side, we've got to do something about it and you're it.

Back from France, through a great season in the national championship with Wellington, and now into my first North-South match with a team to be selected for a full tour of the British Isles. I am trying to build from number eight the sort of relationship Mourie sketched out that night in Auch. But as a pack we are getting cleaned out by one of those well-drilled, grafting, non-stop South Island efforts.

All the character in the world, these South Islanders. I hate to think of them getting into some sort of secession syndrome because some North Islanders think New Zealand stops at the Bombay Hills and others think it stops at Cook Strait. Quite outside rugby, South Islanders have a warmth and innate sense of courtesy which sets them apart. Just at the moment in 1978 though, the South Island forwards aren't quite what the Shorter Oxford defines as "courteous"; plainly, we have to do something about it and the logical thing to do is to win more ball. So Mourie and Burke designate seven at the lineout as the place to do it.

Andy Dalton is the thrower — even in those days a matchless timer and placer of the lineout throw — and with my height I am able to go up beyond Wayne Graham and Ash McGregor and give Dave Loveridge the clean possesion to dictate terms. North Island comes away

Andy Dalton . . . the throw-in perfectionist.

in the second spell to win 29-13.

The rugby player at trial and inter-island level who says he does not harbour hope of being an All Black usually lies. The one who says he does not have ambitions to be an All Black does not deserve to be there. In 1978 I had both. The ambition was always there. The hope was strong because of what I had been able to achieve for North Island with that change of strategy. I have said already that I was disappointed when I missed selection and increasingly so as the success of the tour unfolded and one of the number eights virtually sat the tour out.

It was more than that, too. France was to tour in 1979. I'd have given much to have had the opportunity on an extended tour to force some sort of claim for a test against my old club opponents — Joinel, especially — and my Agen friends Daniel Dubroca and Christian Beguerie. As the tour by France eventuated Joinel and Dubroca were key figures in a second-test turn-up which enabled France to square the series. In that match Gary Seear played his 11th successive test at number eight for the All Blacks, living proof that the selectors recognised the need for height at the back — but not so acutely a year before that they were prepared to select two tall men for a long tour. Seear went on to play his 12th in the one-off match against Australia at Sydney but in the confection of international rugby in 1979 they found a place for me — an exotic experience and an educational one playing against Argentina.

It was here that Ken Stewart showed me that in commitment at the most extreme level he had much the same attitude as Graham Williams. Hugo Porta always seemed to have so much room to create his uncanny advances. But he **was** the Argentina backline. Eric Watson, a great man for detail, studied Porta. He absorbed the elusiveness of the man, his ability to turn as tight as a matador, to beat a man, to spin and go the other way, to break a tackle. There was — and is — such beauty in Porta, such a range of artistry that it would take a finely-devised strategy to lock him in a vaccuum tank, away from his backline, lopped off from his forwards. Porta's centre of gravity is low-slung at any time but approaching the tackle he almost squats in his run as he presents hip and thigh to the tackler, maintaining his own balance and using the tackler for leverage.

Watson decided that even if it cost both Kenny and me we had to control Porta. It was not as if we would starve Porta of ball. Argentina had immense men in the forwards, the Iachetti brothers at 6ft 9 and 6ft 7, Travaglini at much the same size. They lost the lineouts but they really contested. Kenny and I worked on it. Kenny would have a crack at Porta while always making sure he forced him one way. Being as fast and aggressive as he was Kenny disconcerted Porta, often forcing him into my arms. Once, from a lineout, Kenny forced him to me and I took him into touch. Porta smiled and patted my head. It was, in its way, a concession that no man, not even one as rare as Porta, is a rugby team.

The Argentines won all their provincial matches except that against Counties and it was the strongest indication that before long the country would severely press any rugby nation in the world.

New Zealand trial, 1979. No contest — Gary Seear and I both winners.

Eric Watson, the coach who took me through my first All Black experiences, will never overwhelm a stranger with natural bonhomie or effusiveness. Eric has a pinched, suspicious look about him which says "take no one at face value". It's natural caution carried to Caledonian extremes and if you react pompously or with resentment to it he slots you away in a mental filing cabinet under "S" for "Smartarse".

It took me time to settle with Eric. I spoke with him for the first time in our Wellington hotel the day before the second test against

Argentina. He was, shall we say, blunt: "You're a bit of a smartarse, Mexted, aren't you?" I started to feel a bit old-fashioned toward Eric at that instant. He wasn't finished. "I've heard about you. You think you're bloody good, don't you?"

I said something like, "Eric, I've never spoken to you before this moment."

"No, that's right. But I know all about you. I've got you worked out."

I told him I didn't think he was being very fair, which on immediate reflection seemed an inadequate response.

Later he approached me, looking quizzically at my jacket. He was elaborately fastidious as he brushed imaginary specks from my lapels with the tips of his fingers . . . "I know you city boys with your little collars and smartarse ways, heads up in the rucks, easily bruised. Not like the **real** guys. Kenny (Stewart), Leicester (Rutledge). No questions. Heads down and **in**to it . . ." and his eyes screwed up and his flattened hand swooped low, like a fighter pilot describing a pass against the Red Baron . . . "**In**to it!"

By now Eric Watson was coming into focus. He was a player of head-games. Much, much shrewder than often he was given credit for. He probed for the softest spot in a player's ego and scratched it . . . "An All Black forward from **Wellington?** We're looking for **tough** forwards — forwards like the South Island guys, **men** of the **land** . . ."

Long after Argentina, in the public bar of our pub in Swansea during the 1980 tour leading to the match celebrating 100 years of Welsh rugby, Eric approached Stu Wilson and me. It was the heavy psychologist again . . . "There's a test match coming up you know. If you don't have a good game here you're gone. Geoff Old's playing bloody well."

He could still prick me into arrogance. I told him if I didn't think I was the best number eight around I wouldn't be there.

Eric went quiet and stared at me. Abruptly he turned to Stu. "You hotshot Wellingtonians, you're all the same." But it was without rancour, delivered with a sort of self-satisfied affection. He had taken his point, he felt.

I developed a genuine liking for Eric Watson. The city boy from Wellington who bruised easily learned to take the taunts for what they were. I have sent him postcards when I'm away on tour.

I toured with him first to Scotland and England in 1979, my first All Black tour. There had been a sense of unreality about climbing into full All Black uniform for the matches against Argentina. It was as if it were some sort of sham. The New Zealand teams for the two tests were selected only from players who had not played in the two

Eric Watson . . .
player of headgames.

My first game for New Zealand — against Argentina, 1979. The start of the number eight-halfback combination with Dave Loveridge.

official tests against France and though there was pride in it there was a gnawing in a corner of the mind which reminded you that out there, not eligible, were 16 players who were **real** All Blacks.

But Scotland and England! The silver fern meant everything I had dreamed it would mean — and more. Much more. Eric decided at one stage I was riding too high. It offended his devoutly-held creed that smartarses must not assume vainglorious ways just before a test match.

I had scored a try in the opening match of the tour against London Division at Twickenham. Then another against Midland Division at Leicester. And another in the test against Scotland. Against South and South-West Counties at Exeter, four days before the test against England, I had made some pretty damaging runs and I was thinking this international rugby was a piece of cake. Eric decisively removed cake from the menu. Immediately after the match, he said, "Would you like me to get you your own ball so the others can have a game, too?" It made me feel what I was: a tyro international, high on some good runs in what had been a pretty dreadful team performance. Eric knew the time to cut back on self-congratulation.

The much-exhibited try I scored against Scotland was put down by Scottish commentators as a great piece of opportunism, but it was an "Andy Dalton original". Scotland had Alan Tomes and David Gray at 3 and 5 in the lineout. Both were very tall men and we were battling to win the volume of ball we wanted. Half an hour into the game Mourie changed tactics. Haden and I became a two-man lineout. We had not concentrated any practice on it but Dalton, that impeccable thrower, brought credibility to it by throwing with such precision that the two-man lineouts began paying off.

Early in the second spell Andy said to me, "You should have a go from one of these lineouts." The thought hadn't occurred to me but it seemed a hell of a great idea. When we were 35 yards from the Scotland line on our throw I told Dalton I'd balk backward, run forward for his throw just over Haden's head. My marker Ian Lambie snatched the bait. The throw was perfect as I feinted back and ran forward. I had it in my hands, went through the gap and past a surprised scrum-half, Alan Lawson, beat a couple of flatfooted props and bolted. As I neared the line I had a glimpse of the opposite winger, Bruce Hay, coming across like a train but under such momentum that it was easy to evade him and dive over.

Andy Dalton told me he was right at my shoulder screaming for the ball. I heard nothing. My mind was filled with the desire — the **need** — to get to the line. Now **this** was being an All Black, this planned

First tour, second try coming up — against Midland Counties at Leicester, Nigel Horton giving chase.

The Mourie 7-8 philosophy . . . the tackle, free the ball, feed the support . . . London Counties, Twickenham, 1979.

tactic, this smooth understanding between Dalton and me, this realisation that our opposition was hooked, this final rush of elation filling the chest and the mind.

It was not a great All Black team, that 1979 group. It had been lacerated and left unstitched by the unavailability of Gary Knight, Bill Osborne, Bryan Williams, John Ashworth, Lyn Jaffray and then came a dreadful blow with the withdrawal, injured, of Bruce Robertson. When we went in against Scotland six of us were playing our first tests.

But the tour sharpened my understanding of the difference between rugby at that level and all other rugby. The 80 minutes were over in five. The pace of the game imposed new stresses on the mind as well — to think swiftly at least and to hone the mind into instinctive response at best. Instinctively reacting to do the right thing . . . there is the key, the difference between the player who merits a few games for the All Blacks and the one who plays many more. A rugby country like ours has many players who never quite made it, who find their way into those cynical pub-games of selecting All Black teams from all those almost-forgotten names. The instinct for the game and the response of the reactive system to it: it is why the French as a rugby entity are superlatively good striking at high speed and forever with support. It is why New Zealanders are superlatively good in close-quarter advances with intensive support.

I dwell here on Eric Watson because as my first All Black coach he had a special influence on my career. But it was when he was in harness with Mourie that he most confidently approached team coaching. He was rather stereotyped otherwise, too constricted in style and pattern. And it was here that Mourie's perception was of great help to him.

When we went to Australia the following season without Mourie, playing on fields foreign to much of Eric's coaching experience, the need for a freer rein became obvious. We were playing on hard grounds against good positive opposition and Eric persisted with setting up rucks when there should have been acceptance that in these conditions we should be spreading our wings. It was an almost tunnel-visioned approach, a compulsion to slow down the game to control. And there was, of course, the inexplicable self-imposed handicap of going to Australia without Bruce Robertson — the greatest selection blunder of my time.

The Australian end of an increasingly regular rugby relationship with New Zealand has yet to find itself in such things as the hospitality business. They do not lack in hospitable people. They do lack in the pro-

Bruce Robertson . . . called up too late after selection blunder.

vision of adequate accommodation and in their attitude to what their guests might fairly expect in food and in recreation off the field.

We have now such a conglomeration of rugby exchanges with Australia at every level that in pure rugby spin-off both countries prosper. Australian forward play has developed astonishingly in the last decade. New Zealand backplay, of necessity, has sharpened its edge to compete on hard grounds. It is good for the game, too, that contact at international level has become so competitive, the standard of play so even. At this stage I guess New Zealand backs have reached Australian standard and that our forwards hold an edge in technique and in attitude.

This comes from our traditional grounding, the built-in need we have to produce ball while going forward. We have a consistency of attitude which the Australians do not yet match, but nor do most teams in the world.

The tour of 1980 typifies what I feel about touring Australia and it is a feeling shared by many All Blacks. We know the rugby is going to be hard and enjoyable in Queensland and New South Wales. We know the pace of the game will be testing, but we welcome that, too. But there is little recognition by the Australian Rugby Union that touring teams deserve accommodation of good quality and that penny-pinching on food and such basic things as laundry is skinflint mentality on a tour generating big money. I have talked to players who were there in 1968 and they recall with disgust the restrictions placed on food availability in Brisbane and the standard of accommodation and food across Sydney Harbour at Manly and how their manager, Duncan Ross of North Auckland, hammered for at least reasonable concern from the Australian Union.

Things have not improved. In 1984 we battled continually with the liaison officer over food. We were not asking for cordon bleu, we didn't even want full a la carte selection. We did want good food with some variety. That is not being unduly precious. There is a constant outpouring of energy by a touring team and the players, especially the forwards, need sufficient and good food.

The attitude toward laundry was archaic. We were asked by the liaison officer to wash our own socks and underwear to cut back on the laundry bill.

I look from the extreme of plenty to the extreme of want — from Australia to Romania. Romania is deprived. In Romania they queue for soap, for flour, for salt. They rarely speak openly for fear of some reprisal. We toured Romania in 1981. It was an experience. It was not an experience any of us would want soon again. Deprivation and depression in what once was a beautiful, extroverted nation do not make for touring contentment. We were conscious that what we ate and drank was often hard come-by and not available to the "ordinary" citizenry. But the rugby people of Romania strove desperately to supply us with food in quantity and of a quality they themselves could little afford.

All Blacks have the impression Australian administrators do not put themselves out to ensure a touring team lives reasonably well. In this, they do not do justice to their own players. It is inevitable that the sort of dissatisfaction the administrators' attitude engenders in a touring team will rub off on player relationships. The competitiveness between the two countries is healthy. The atmosphere is not. It is cool and I blame it almost entirely on the Australian Rugby Union. There is sufficient goodwill among the players to mend the fracture if the union would do its part as well, say, as the New Zealand Rugby Union in its approach to touring players.

Players do not look for luxury. New Zealanders are pretty basic. But they do look for common courtesies as guests. For all the criticisms we may have of the French attitude at times they do set out with pride to entertain teams at such magnificent shows as the Lido, the Follies, at some of the fine estate vineyards. They organise trips to the Louvre, to Notre Dame, the Pigalle, the Eiffel Tower . . . the point is that they plan it and do it. The Australians have no Louvre or Lido, of course. But what they have got is a magnificent country. I wish they would expose it to us.

Australia should be one of the most desirable tours of all. We are aligned in so many ways. We are now aligned in our organisation of the first World Cup of rugby and that was not achieved without a whole heap of aggro, either. No one actually committed grievous bodily harm but the knives were flashing. When it was all over and the arrangements announced a point was made of emphasising that, through it all, New Zealand and Australian rugby had emerged with a warm new understanding of each other.

I hope that is right, in every respect. Having reached this warm new understanding I hope the administrators will recognise that the players could do with some warm new understanding, too, so that after a tour of Australia we will not have senior players saying they will not be fighting to go back. With guys like Simon Poidevin, Nick Farr-Jones, Andy Slack and Roger Gould — and others, too — fraternising among the players should be warmer than between the players of any other two countries. But there's a mutually-erected barrier and that is a tragedy for rugby.

There is respect in New Zealand for the quality of the Australian game. We were thoroughly beaten on the 1980 tour — and the mystery food poisoning before the final test is not an excuse. The Wallabies had our measure, they recognised the limitations in our tactical approach, and they exploited them brilliantly. Coming from a winning first year as an All Black in Scotland and England and from my second off-season with Agen I anticipated that tour eagerly. Hungrily, even. For many reasons I felt flattened by the experience. No player likes to go home from a losing tour but that was only a fragment of it. If you were to multiply my disenchantment by that of at least half the team you would have a damned good reason to sort out urgently phase two of the "warm, new understanding" because nothing has changed.

I can envisage the Aussies' reaction to this. If it is true to form they will discard everything I have said as sensationalist, exaggerated, designed to sell books, designed to further splinter the ANZUS Pact, designed to stir up the public virtually on the eve of a full Australian tour to New Zealand. I can only hope, I suppose, that at least one enlightened administrator will read it and take from it with concern the message within it.

Australian rugby means more to me than hard contest and the continuing flow of tests played at maximum speed. There is a lasting memory for me, too, of one of the finest of all individuals I have played against. Mark Ella retired when I judged him to be at the peak of his skill for he seemed to me to improve every time I played against him. In the early matches he was just good. At the end he was magnificent. He added shrewdness to his extraordinary ball skills, balance and rhythm.

For me, as a defender, he posed special problems. He carried the ball so low it was impossible to predict whether he intended to pass, dummy or drop it on his foot. The advantage he had over the pre-1985 Porta was that he had fine players outside him and we could not afford to designate a defence on him alone. Ella could make so much from nothing and I am sorry he has adorned international rugby for such a comparatively short span.

Wales and the whistlers

When Nicky Allen played his second and last rugby test for the All Blacks he was expressing in his own whimsical way that rugby is a game of beauty, like life. And, like life, for living. It was appealing that Nicky should be playing that sort of rugby in a land which rather takes to itself the right to produce fly-halves (or first five-eighths) of ethereal quality. So much so that they compose poems about such things as "fly-half factories", and make gilt models of Barry John's boots, Phil Bennett's jockstrap and Cliff Morgan's kneecaps. Fly-half play is the religion of Wales.

The tour of North America and Wales in 1980 was set up as a challenge. Thank you, for North America, which was seen as an occasion for the team to settle in before the extraordinary schedule devised for it in Wales. The Welsh were saying, "Come, All Blacks. We want you for our centennial celebrations. But when you run on to the Arms Park for the big one you're going to know you've already been in a hell of a tour. So good luck, but don't hold your breath." And the New Zealand Rugby Union was saying to the Welsh, "We accept".

And that was the mood of the players as they faced up to a tour which went, Cardiff, Llanelli, Swansea, Newport, Wales — and all in the space of two weeks. The Welsh regarded the itinerary with satisfaction. We regarded it as nice piece of Welsh engineering. Eric Watson regarded it, as was his want, with deep suspicion. And then, with Graham Mourie, set about a plan to win not just the celebratory test of Welsh rugby but every game on the tour. The manager, Ray Harper, told a cynical army of pressmen — most of them Fleet Street ferrets — that the prime aim of the tour was to cement the good relations between the Welsh and the New Zealanders.

I suspect we might better have achieved that had we lost with grace at Cardiff Arms for that vast Welsh crowd stopped singing historically early and when they stop singing early at Cardiff Arms the cementing of good relations usually stops with it. The Welsh love of rugby glows like a beacon on a black night. The Welsh love of winning glows yet brighter.

Some of the All Blacks had savoured the power of the Welsh rugby atmosphere previously when touring with Mourie's grand-slammers. To me Wales was the history in Billy Wallace's wrinkled hands and bright eyes. It was the history in the sepia-tone photograph of the 1924 Invincibles on my wall at home. It was the country which had saturated the New Zealand rugby psyche since 1905, the country we wanted to beat more than any other. Except South Africa. But that's different.

If only New Zealand rugby had expressed itself at the Sydney Cricket Ground four months earlier as it did that day at Cardiff, and as it did throughout Wales. If only there had been a rallying figure like Mourie. If only . . . But Eric Watson nominated the All Blacks' tactics for Wales before we left home — "Make no mistake," he said, "this team is going to run the ball in Wales." So it did and the Welsh teams had neither the wit nor the desire to run it back at us.

And Nicky Allen scored a try against Wales. Nicky would have made Pierre Lacroix cry. His gift was such that Barry John wept for it that day. Balance, rhythm, timing. The **instinct.** They were as much a part of Nicky as his wanderlust spirit and his need for fun. We were training at Porthcawl, out there by the sea, and Eric Watson was giving a team talk. Nicky put the ball on his head and stood as if it were as snug there as a beret. As Eric talked Nicky started bouncing the ball — head-knee-nose-elbow-arm-knuckles-ankle-chest-foot-head. Eric said testily, "Are you listening to me?" Nicky missed not a beat. He bounced the ball off his bum back to his elbow and went into a new routine while repeating word for word the wisdom of Eric.

Nicky was an audacious little guy. He attracted ladies without trying — a talent greatly envied by other young men in the party. At 21 he infected older players with his freedom of spirit; there was no duplicity in him and they sensed, too, there was no false obsequiousness. They were drawn to him as a friend.

Nicky died in 1984. He was just 26. At his funeral his friend Steve Creadus said, "It's as if he knew he was going to die young and he was trying to fit two lives into one."

Guys like Haden, Loveridge, Shaw and me still sit around and talk about Nicky — and the jokes flow. It's Nicky entertaining us all over

Nicky Allen . . . the blithe spirit of rugby.

Sad day. Nicky Allen's funeral.

again. He was going to come to Wellington to flat with me in the city. He would have adorned Wellington rugby and he would have destroyed any credibility I might have had as an emerging responsible citizen.

I still get this uncanny feeling; the hair at the back of my neck bristles. Nicky is going to put his head over my shoulder again and say, "C'mon, Fizz. Let's go."

After the test against Wales Cliff Morgan paid an eloquent tribute to Mourie. "When I was a lad," he said, "down in Llanelli old men used to say, 'Now I can go happily to my maker because I have seen Albert Jenkins play.' After today's win by the All Blacks over Wales I do not mind going to **my** maker because today I saw, from Graham Mourie, the greatest looseforward display the world could ever wish to see."

And, yes, it was vintage Mourie. I would take another loose forward from that match and nominate his performance as memorable in a completely different way, a way Mark (Cowboy) Shaw has made his own in world rugby. Where Mourie had the Welsh at their poetry Shaw had them stunned with the velocity of his game that day. I have played in only a few test matches without Shaw at blindside flank and at number six in the lineouts. There were two in 1979 before his advent, one in Australia when Bryce Rope preferred a Frank Shelford who was rampantly in form, the third against the Springboks in 1981. But however illogical it may seem I cannot bring tangible form to playing a test match without him.

Shaw projects to the rugby public and to the media a mixture they find difficult to rationalise. There is acceptance of his remarkable ability as a bursting, driving, close-supporting tight-loose forward. None better. There is also the Shaw dishing out rough justice — and sometimes rough injustice. Where softball has its designated hitter it seems rugby has its Cowboy Shaw. But I suggest 90 per cent of the incidents in which Shaw becomes involved stem from his compulsion to sort out other players' troubles. He is quick to retaliate on someone else's behalf. I suppose you could call him a sorter-out.

Shaw has this overwhelming sense of loyalty to his friends, to his team and to his country. If he was in a working-bee raising club funds and there were three jobs left — shifting sand, shifting topsoil or cleaning the bog — Cowboy would volunteer to clean the bog just to save his mates doing it. The bruising macho-image of Shaw under a full head of steam on the field is not the Shaw his fellow-players know off the field. He is quiet and has a completely natural sense of courtesy and decency. Peter Bush, whose rugby pictures have world recognition,

Mark Shaw, showing his other side, one with a natural sense of courtesy and decency.

caught Shaw in an act of old-world charm in the middle of downtown New Plymouth before the North-South match in 1985. A frail old lady, partly blind and feeling her way with a white stick, stood on the kerb-side as the traffic rolled. She was uncertain, tentative. Cowboy went to her, took her arm and, holding one forbidding hand up to the traffic, he walked her gently across the street.

Wales suited him. He responded strongly to the almost blind faith of the Welsh in their players to beat anyone — and most of all us at Cardiff. We would be "beat" by Cardiff and failing that we would be "beat" by Llanelli or Swansea or Newport. Cowboy absorbed it all. The night before the test we watched on television a programme covering the history of Welsh rugby, its grandeur, its holiness almost.

It suited Cowboy's preparation perfectly. By the time the game started, what with his memory of the past two weeks in Wales, the television programme and the crowd singing, Cowboy was finely tuned. His performance was devastating.

We felt great as a team that day. We aimed to stop the crowd singing at the earliest possible moment. JPR Williams said at the dinner that night, "I can't believe it. We weren't even in it." At 23-3 it was true.

For myself, the Wales tour brought more fine tuning of my particular instrument in the All Black band. Undoubtedly I was contributing more, very much in the play. Now there was the instinctive floating to the point of contact with the ball, the clear view of my support and the time to distribute. With Mourie in such wonderful touch my shadowing of him became a consistent source of profit for the All Blacks. In this there was such satisfaction as I had not till then experienced.

The referee for that match was John West of Ireland. Where are the John Wests of Home Unions refereeing now? Gone to pasture everyone — and taken with them the generous minds which are essential to the continuing vitality of rugby. When I was first in Britain, in 1979, it was a delight to play under referees who wanted to referee the game **for** the game. None was better in this than West. Things have changed dramatically for the worse and to the detriment of British rugby.

Fluency has gone and with it entertainment. The referees are down on their knees looking for a reason to blow the whistle. British rugby has always been held up by tradition as the creme de la creme — the swift movement of the ball through the threequarters, the wings scoring the tries, the epitome of all that was fine in rugger.

But the wheel has turned. Home Unions teams may strive to emerge from the rut into which their rugby has collapsed and in any circumstances that would take a long time. In these special circumstances where the referees have taken such an egotistical stance in the game it will take longer than it should. The Irish may come through with some fine running — or the Scots. But the strangulating influence of the referees, interpreting tomes of laws to the letter, leaves British rugby sitting squarely on the penalty goal — the overwhelming factor which once it despised.

As their referees have tugged on the reins, ours have become more worldly-wise, less clinical, and that is to their everlasting credit. The lesson is clear. It is no coincidence that the standard of rugby in the British Isles has deteriorated as the mentality of refereeing has become more miserable. Nor that our backplay has improved markedly as our referees have developed understanding.

As a player I hate over-officious referees, men who search for a reason to blow the whistle as though oblivious to the movement and spirit of the game. Mine is typical, I believe, of the attitude of New Zealand players.

I have great respect for Australian referees, and especially Kerry Fitzgerald. I have had less respect for them in the past when they have controlled matches with the Wallabies. Australians are faced with a stern contest for the public's dollar and it becomes vital for rugby union to provide a spectacle attractive to the sporting masses. Australian referees take their "home" attitude out into the international market and their freedom of thought, without insult to the game's most cardinal laws, should be circulated as a model tutorial to the rest of the world. Had there been an Australian referee for the two-test series against France in New Zealand in 1984 we would have had bonanza-rugby for the people. Both teams wanted to move the ball but Winston Jones, of Wales, brought with him all the fastidious pedantry which is spoiling British rugby.

I have said New Zealand had no excuses for losing the test series in Australia in 1980. I would add to that, nevertheless, that when they were refereeing Wallaby tests Australian referees were as patriotic as South African referees with the Springboks. That tour we had the choice of three referees. One was incompetent. One was overly nationalistic. One was a combination of both.

It is in the nature of French referees to let the game run though sometimes, as in our 1983 match against Scotland at Murrayfield, their intent can be hindered by the skinny mentality of British touch-judges who have taken their right to "flag" incidents as a free-pass to propel themselves into the game. The French are unpredictable, often affected by circumstances and have a deep-seated wish not to upset anyone.

South African refereeing is plainly shocking. Locked out from international experience they go their own way, so many of them governed by the rigid Afrikaner mentality and in the past heavily influenced by the most nationalistic crowds in world rugby.

Referees say they are in a no-win situation, bound over by masses of laws, under abuse by crowds if there is too much whistle, under abuse by crowds if there is too little whistle and this is seen to affect the result, under abuse by players who want rhythm and consistency in the game, under abuse by their peers who judge them. I believe that overwhelmingly the most valid of these is the volume of the laws. This crowds the referees' mind to the detriment of all else. It leads to the most in-

Clive Norling . . . a centre-stage referee.

sidious of all influences in refereeing — that if he has not seen an offence there is bound to have been one anyway — and it suffocates the will of players to open up.

Players favour a reduction in the laws, simplification rather than multiplication, but within that process there should also be introduced a requirement for backs to be ten metres back at scrums as well as at lineouts.

I have reserved my final comment on referees — and, specifically, British referees — for Clive Norling. As I will discuss in detail later the third test against South Africa in 1981 was the single most memorable rugby experience of my life for all manner of reasons. I can say here, though, that it is terribly disconcerting to players to be in a match of that importance with a referee they are scared of. The feeling with Norling was always that if we scored, South Africa would be given a penalty to balance the books, then back to us, then . . . A centre-stage referee like Norling imposes additional pressures in a game — and that test was one game where we needed no stress-input from a man whose job it should simply have been to guide and adjudicate without fuss. Clive Norling could never fit that job-description. He was far too interested in projecting Clive Norling. And on Saturday, September 12, 1981, at Eden Park neither Springboks nor All Blacks needed him.

Surfing, spoofing, South Africa

When I first became an All Black I feared I would not survive long enough to tour South Africa. It's a competitive world out there among the 50 players who might realistically compete for a place among 30. Ruthlessly competitive. And there are fickle flicks of fortune and misfortune — you are at the behest of selectors' whims and fancies, you have to be clear of injury, you may be faced with such business and family responsibilities that touring becomes impossible. All I know is that I wanted **my** day for a crack at the Springboks in their own land. I wanted **my** turn to help show a New Zealand team, carefully selected and properly tuned for the job, could beat them.

Well, I survived for 1985 . . .

But I knew I had to go to South Africa long, long before I became an All Black — and it had nothing to do with rugby. It had to do with a glossy magazine, a coloured picture of Jeffreys Bay and a New Zealand kid who couldn't stay away from the sea.

When I was 13 I read a book called Men Who Ride Mountains. It was about the big waves of Hawaii, of Waimea Bay and Sunset Beach on the north shore. I was a pretty busy kid in those days, riding surf of a couple of feet out at Raumati Beach on the Kapiti Coast, north of Wellington. Riding surf! Well, two foot waves are a pretty big deal when you are skinny and little and your board is a big, heavy job which sits in the sea like a plank. I was so light I could paddle the wave and the board would hardly move. But for all that, this to me was a magical world.

Adventure runs swiftly in the blood of most kids. Men Who Ride Mountains quickened my sense of adventure. I wanted bigger waves and more excitement. I was into every surfing publication I could find, and one day I saw the pictures of Jeffreys Bay tucked away in the Eastern Cape of South Africa. I have never forgotten it. I was fascinated by the beauty of it, by the vivid blue of the sea and the long run of big waves. There, that long ago, I really began my search for "Bruce's Beauties", the perfect surfing wave named after the American surf-guru Bruce Brown, who recognised the consistent and exceptional shape of them from the sandhills above, the lines of perfect waves peeling off like lines of corduroy. St Francis Bay, the great sweep in which Jeffreys Bay nestles back to the west, catches the Beauties at its Cape and Jeffreys Bay harbours the surfing area known as Supertubes.

At 15, that to me was South Africa — a land of white beaches, fantastic right-breaks and hardly anyone surfing. Idyllic. I would get there. Rugby? Rugby had nothing to do with it.

At the same age, with three friends, I loaded four surfboards on the roof-rack of an Austin Cambridge — the old A60 — and we disappeared out of Wellington in a cloud of hot summer dust. My friends were Neil Gardiner, now a potter, Peter Brady, a Golden Bay park ranger, and Ken Allen, a P and T linesman in Nelson County. What followed was nearly three months of life no surf-mad, sun-mad teenager could ever forget. We travelled from beach to beach, we slept in a tent, in the car, by the side of the road, in empty sections. We trekked over miles of farmland to find a beach here and another there. We ate sumptuously from the cornfields of unknowingly generous farmers and we drank cold beer while trying to look less under-age than we were.

First we "did" the west coast, surfing the beautiful beaches through the Taranaki coast. We "discovered" Raglan and got blown apart by big, powerful waves, 10 feet of heaving west coast waves which dissuaded us from trying them for the first two days. We looked a lot. And we talked with nervous bravado a lot as we glanced sideways at all those rocks. Then finally we rode them, those big lefts, beautiful long waves — but for the first time I understood how awesome the sea is . . . getting caught inside and trying to get out past the white water . . . getting smashed by the waves, coming up to another, trying to ride it hanging under the board but finding no compromise, no compassion from the sea . . . a board lost, a battering on the rocks, bruises, abrasions . . . try again.

Getting out past white water, exhausted, behind you the big ones loom, frightening — but to get on them! Ecstasy. Every time I catch a wave there's a rush of the same passion. At 32 nothing's changed. Except understanding, being paddling-fit, agile, reactive to what the wave does, learning that each wave has its own character. Even when

Those were the days. The first surfing expedition, 1968: with Ken Allen, Neil Gardiner, Peter Brady and the less trusty Austin Cambridge.

you get that one magnificent wave and go through your entire repertoire there is still more to be done. The possibilities are limitless.

As a 15-year-old you become engrossed. When you come out of the water to rest you turn back to watch the waves and you dream. At night you go back out to the beach and stare at them and you imagine what you'd do on "that" wave and you go to sleep dreaming of it. Next morning, the shock of cold water from a warm sleeping bag, the race to get the first wave . . .

From Raglan across to Mount Maunganui . . . smaller waves, more girls; friendly waves, friendly girls. A new dimension to surfing. Some of the bathing suits never got wet. Every day was in the water, on the beach, under the sun. That period at Mount Maunganui locked itself in my mind and I would never want to be distant from the sea and the T-shirt-and-shorts life.

Through to the north and 90-mile Beach, back across to the east coast and the ultimate experience on a board. At 15 I got tubed for the first time. Wainui Beach, Gisborne, 6 am, a nice offshore breeze holding the waves up. They were tubing. Perfect tubes. We had seen it in magazines and surf movies but never experienced it. It was time. I paddled out, caught my wave, and got tubed, crouching low, like being in a tunnel, roaring toward the opening at the end, I sat down low and tubed, just me in a wave on a board. I got this amazing rush of blood, enveloped by the sea but untouched, exploiting the power of it, washed in the strange light of it . . .

Years later when I was playing rugby with Agen, my first season, having success, pleasing the administrators, pleasing the crowds, I was asked to go on a skiing trip with four Frenchmen and five French girls. The timing was bad but the experience promised so much that I organised myself. I had to make the four-hour drive to Limoges to meet the party and that meant leaving the field in Agen before full time.

I have always had this shoulder that cracks. A good, big satisfying crack and no harm done. A few minutes before time I grabbed my shoulder, looked suitably agonised, groaned but didn't go into "French convulsions" so they knew I must really be injured. They heard my shoulder do its crunch act and panicked. Hospital, hospital, Murree must go to hospital. Hospital I didn't need but I was bundled away, doctors listened to my shoulder and expressed themselves as being intensely interested in having a go at it. Fix it for good, they said, waving scalpels all over the place. I exited forcibly, ran to my car and drove to Limoges and from there to Val d'Isere.

On a chairlift I met a French-Canadian and as we neared the top I saw that a lone skier had cut a beautiful pattern in the powder-snow. He had walked up a mile beyond the lift limit to take full, sweeping advantage of the slope and the snow. I said, "I'll bet that guy had a hell of a great time." He said, "Yes. I did. Skiing that virgin snow was better than an orgasm."

Better than an orgasm. Wainui Beach that early morning so many years before. For a few seconds I was in that tube again. He was right.

My youth in the sea was not all tubing, friendly girls and sunbathing. A year after Wainui I was among big left breaks out in Lyall Bay on Wellington's rocky southern coast. The sea snatched my board and hurled me under, tossed me like a salad until I didn't know where up was and where down. I swam for space and hit the bottom. I panicked and after an age came out of it, took a heaving gasp of salt spray and was hit by another big one and towed under. I knew I was going to drown. Then, with the roar in my ears, it spewed me up contemptuously into the shallows.

Years later there was the close call in the 28-footer Kidnapper in Cook Strait, sailing for home from the Marlborough Sounds. I was on the helm and we were doing 11 or 12 knots under the spinnaker. It was all too damned casual. Suddenly, we broached. I lost contact and the yacht went crazy. Everyone was hanging on. We couldn't get the sails down. It was dark and there were girls and guys hanging on to ropes all over the place. Finally, we motored out of it, righted ourselves, set sail again and headed off in precisely the wrong direction. The Sea 4, us 0.

Surfing is the most challenging sport I have ever been involved with, and the most exhilarating. There is no other person to beat, no team,

Spoofing at the New Zealand High Commissioner's residence in Suva in 1984. From left, High Commissioner Lindsay Watt, Andy Haden, Barry Sweetman (Fiji's former chairman), John Stevens (New Zealand Trade Commission), David Kirk and me.

no touch judge. The challenge is between you alone and the sea. Triumphs over the sea are transient and they come only in the skirmishing. In the battles which win wars the sea never loses. Thus it commands the deepest respect.

I say this to youngsters who look for their kicks out of gluepots or on the end of reefers: there's no bigger kick, no greater high than having it off with the sea. In this country the sea laps closely everywhere. Get into it.

The rugby pull to South Africa became strong in 1976 when my father followed Andy Leslie's All Blacks through the country. His experiences added to my growing consciousness that there could be a future for me in rugby - and that meant South Africa. I was playing for Wellington, edging toward a New Zealand trial. These things were a beginning. The stories my father brought home sharpened ambition to see for myself and one day to wear black on to Loftus Versfeld, King's Park, Ellis Park, Boet Erasmus, Newlands, Free State Stadium, names that rang of rugby.

Factor three had nothing to do with surfing, something to do with rugby and a lot to do with the ancient and honourable art of spoofing.

Spoofing is defined in the encyclopedia of sport and recreation as an ancient art of mental calculation played among gentlemen. Spoofing has its imitators, such as the New Zealand pub game of "matches", but spoofing carries things to a state of refinement. It is selective and played in an organised and dignified manner. Spoofers do not get drunk spoofing, unless they play it long enough. Often they play it long enough. In alcohol, spoofers retain their dignity at all times. They maintain a high level of bored humour which never descends to vulgarity or sex. During spoofing decorum is of the utmost, players and bystanders referring to others only by surname and desirably prefixed by Mister. True spoofing is played with coins and true spoofers profit not from spoofing other than in the quaffing of liquor purchased by the loser or from a sedate luncheon or dinner likewise settled by he who lacks the concentration, discipline and incredible acumen to win.

The game, though not the name, is based on a Dutch royal court game of some centuries ago. That, anyway, is what spoofers propose. It involves the assessment of an opponent's mentality, the reading of his mind's deepest deceptions. Each member of the school holds three coins. He presents, hidden in the hand, any number of those coins or none at all. It is in the progressive assessment of the total number of coins held by the school that the art lies.

Spoofing is a fellowship the membership of which is indefinable but universal. I thank with all my heart Mr Nick Poynton, Cambridge University graduate in something, and Mr Bill Endicott, Cambridge University graduate in something else, for introducing me to it. It has brought me new friends all over the world and through our meeting in the James Cook Hotel, Wellington, on the evening of June 17, 1977, I have had experiences in and out of rugby which have brightened my life.

Mr Poynton and Mr Endicott travelled from the other side of the world to follow the 1977 Lions, Mr Poynton from England and Mr Endicott from South Africa where he had lived for eight years. On the evening of June 17, the night before the Lions played New Zealand at Athletic Park, they spoofed around the grand piano in the piano bar of the James Cook. Mr Endicott wore a finely-cut three-piece suit and a safari hat. The spoofing, the spoofing banter and catch-words had American, Japanese, British and New Zealand guests caught up and hugely entertained. When I walked in with my friend Peter Brooks I wondered who this lot thought they were, taking over the town I loved.

Now I have spoofed in half a dozen countries, at championship level, at pub level, at footy level. In France the five call becomes, of course, "cinq", a sound roughly equivalent to "sank". In Argentina the five call became "General Belgrano" because it sank, in New Zealand it became "Wahine" for the same reason and, more recently in Auckland, it became "Rainbow Warrior" because that definitely sank. There is a spoofers' society based in Fiji and there Mr Andrew Haden, Mr Wayne Smith and myself played with the son of the Prime Minister, Ratu Sir Kamasese Mara, and the Tongan Minister of Finance. The Minister of Finance had difficulty with the figures so Mr Haden helped him.

I spoofed around England for two or three weeks leading up to my first stint with Agen and then during that winter went back for Five-Nations championship matches and spoofing at Lansdowne Road, Twickenham and Murrayfield.

Going to Twickers with the spoofing fraternity is something out of Wodehouse. Travel to the ground is by an aged converted double-decker bus with a built-in bar. At the ground, a pint of best bitter before laying out the table in the parking lot. Chicken salad, a little pheasant perhaps, cold Melton pork pies, sandwiches (egg), sandwiches (cucumber). You know, the sort of thing. You do it every Saturday at Fraser Park or the Miramar Polo Ground.

You slip into your seat in time for kick-off and nick out at half-time for a pint.

Mr Poynton and his fellow-spoofers watch rugby as if the players are actors on-stage and they the audience far removed from the realities, the stresses and tensions of the play. They deliberately remove themselves from that sort of proximity to the match yet they know their rugby, quietly make astute comments, yet studiedly distance themselves from it. It is not "on" to become too involved, not "on" emotionally to support England or one's own team lest it affect appreciation of good play from the other side.

Because of my experience of this I can understand the detachment of Rugby Football Union (of England) administrators before an international kick-off. They stroll into the dressing rooms, tap you on the shoulder and say, "Mexted, isn't it? I knew your father, played with him, don't you know, at . . ." And I'm getting ready for a test match and the dressing room has that solid wall of tension about it. But to these people we're just chaps going to play a game of rugger. There is something refreshing about that.

At one time I joined a French team called the Ancient Internationals who were to play an old-age Scottish side in Edinburgh. I was something like a guest player and I was appointed to full-back. It was one of those diverting occasions you would never be without. We were clad in Victorian-style costumes and Mr Poynton was on the crowded touchline shouting to the Scots such advice as "Put him under the high ball! He's very vulnerable!"

I introduced two of the French team to spoofing and we spoofed from pub to pub around Edinburgh for four days — never for profit, of course, just to maintain one's standing with one's fellows! The French loved it.

Spoofing became another good reason for me to spend some time in South Africa on my way home from the first season with Agen. I would tie up with Mr Endicott and, hopefully, I would see for myself the supertubes and caress the sand of Jeffreys Bay. I wanted to get some sort of feel for the country without being pretentious enough to think that in a week or two I could absorb its problems. And there was certainly no way I would pretend to scratch the surface of its policies. The three weeks I had there set the stage for me to go back and I intended to do that quickly because scenically, the country is majestic and, as a sportsman, I found it magnetic.

And Jeffreys Bay was everything I had imagined as a boy, and more. Much more.

I would return soon, I knew. But, in fact, I did not go back to South Africa until 1982 and by then much had happened. The All Blacks had hosted Scotland at the beginning of the 1981 season and had toured Romania and France at the end. While we were playing Scotland at Eden Park (and winning comprehensively), in South Africa a great sweep of trials was under way. The objective of all players in those trials, black and white, was to tour New Zealand. Now, and forever, when people here talk of the rugby year of 1981 the two-test defeat of the Scots is the dimmest memory. The pioneering tour of Romania and the two-test defeat of France are shadowy events which, for recall, require perusal of the histories.

What 1981 means in rugby, in politics, in public trauma will always be the Springboks in New Zealand. The last Springboks in New Zealand for many years and the beginning of the end of the proposed 1985 All Black tour of South Africa.

In hindsight I know many things about South African rugby I did not know in 1981, things which were crammed into my consciousness in the years I played there after that tour, things which affected my own approach to the game — squeezing the French out of my rugby.

The South African game is based on power and force, no broad vision as in the French whose elusiveness and flexibility of mind are just caught sufficiently within game-plan to enhance them. Such is the French mind, of course, that sometimes game-plan is enhancing elu-

With Gary Player during a McCarthy Sigma promotion, Durban, 1982.

siveness and flexibility of mind. But that works, too. Where the French come unstuck is when, perhaps only temporarily, elusiveness, flexibility and game-plan produce error and pressure and they become overly emotional about it and game-plan is forgotten before it has had a chance.

That does not happen with the South Africans. Game-plan is everything. Rigidity of purpose is the vehicle. And that is the result of a national trait which permeates life. The Afrikaner has traditionally based his rugby on strength at the scrum. Scrummaging has been everything to him. Props have been the kings of South African rugby. Piet du Toit has meant more to the South African rugby ego than John Gainsford. And, by the same mentality, a blockhouse of a second five-eighths (or inside centre) like Joggie Jansen is recalled with much warmer affection than a beautifully gifted player like the flyhalf Keith Oxlee. It is simply the nature of the beast.

If the Transvaal team is training and 100 people are watching, 95 are staring grimly into the scrums and five are watching the movement of the backs. In France 99 would be watching the backs and the odd-man out would have turned his back for a moment to urinate in full view of the girls' school next door.

Even playing for Natal, which has by far the most enlightened approach to rugby in the country, I found that if I was carrying the ball and knocked someone over it made a big impression. But if I cleanly beat one or two players with body movement it was seen to be unduly flashy and unworthy of response. When, later, I played for the Wanderers Club in Johannesburg this was even more apparent but I do believe I left Wanderers some sort of legacy and that they were playing the game with much more open minds when I left. For instance, I introduced them to the All Blacks' "lefto", where the half-back runs wide to the left from a scrum, the number eight detaches, draws the opposing half-back, passes under his arms and, with the right sort of management, the try is on at the left-hand corner. The team loved it. The spectators scratched their heads, appreciated the four points but could not understand the expertise needed to bring it all about. They were much more in favour of seeing me run wham-bam into the opposing flanker to create a ruck.

Incidentally, the scrum-half for Wanderers was John Robbie, who came to New Zealand with the 1976 Irish team — a young university student with a remarkably quick and wide pass. He has settled in South Africa, become a most accomplished player and, in fact, wore the Springbok jersey, inside Naas Botha, in 1985.

Pre-season training for the Wanderers: much running, sit-ups, press-ups, much more running. "Where," I asked, "is the bloody ball?" The ball, they said, would come when we were fit. Ballwork secondary; no basketball with a rugby ball, none of the ball games which bring such familiarity, such second-nature skill in handling. The great Welsh fly-half, Barry John, stood off and watched the 1971 Lions doing their physical work, not remotely interested in doing strength exercises. "Why should I spend all that time doing push-ups?" he asked. "I might end up as the fly-half with the biggest muscles in the world and the smallest skill repertoire."

There are no Bruce Robertsons or Nicky Allens in South African rugby. There are Bernie Frasers — and that is no disrespect to Bernie, because a Bernie at his peak would have been magnificent in an All Black team touring South Africa. But his sort of strength-pace winger is not uncommon there.

I have never doubted that Errol Tobias, the Coloured midfield back, has been shamefully misused because he does not fit snugly into the utilitarian South African design. Certainly he has the skills. And the Coloured centre Wilfred Cupido, a rhythmic, thrustful runner, not unlike Steve Pokere, was seen to lack the robustness necessary for that

John Robbie, left, and Naas Botha, who formed the Springbok inside back combination in 1985.

stolid sort of Springbok image.

The South African game has become a desperate clinging to the kicking fly-half — the Naas Botha, who can kick into position for the shot at goal or the power-try — and the brick-outhouse centres who can knock over the opposition with kamikaze tackling and mix it with the forwards. Of course, there are notable exceptions — players like Carel du Plessis, who has become a great footballer — but the provincial teams are laden with backs with no ability to beat a man other than by running through him.

It is an inherent narrow-mindedness which afflicts South African rugby and it is compounded by the isolation it suffers.

These things I have learned since 1981, though the signs were there to read then as well. Most significantly they were there in the first test when, afflicted by acute myopia, the touring selection panel decided it would be a hell of a good idea to drop the touring captain, Wynand Claassen, a thinking footballer, an experienced captain but suffering from advanced liberalism. What has emerged since the tour, much of it written evidence from Claassen himself, indicates clearly that had he been one of the "broeders", that hard-nosed tier of Afrikaner elitism, he would have led his team on to Lancaster Park. As it was, Theuns Stofberg, nominated by Claassen as having broederbond connections, captained the team and did it with notable mediocrity.

Claassen's revelations in his book More than Just Rugby, published in 1985, led immediately to his dismissal from the Springbok selection panel but they were endorsed in principle by Dr Danie Craven to whom Claassen referred the book before publication . . . "There may well have been a broeder conspiracy present in the 1981 Springbok team," Claassen wrote. "Johan Claassen (the manager), Nelie Smith (the coach), Theuns Stofberg and Gerrie Germishuys (players) had broeder connections in common."

So in spite of all the movement within rugby to achieve mixed trials and merit selection there are insidious influences which inject the game with political bias. Considering the immense strides taken in a short space of time to open up what once was the closed shop of Springbok trial and selection that is a tragedy. Claassen's exposure of it to public scrutiny at home and abroad must in the short term be an embarrassment to the South African Rugby Board. However, it has achieved something Dr Craven will welcome because he has worked incessantly to ensure the broeder presence on the board should not reach a position of such power that liberal thought is lost to it. There is the strongest suggestion that this is the main reason why in old age he has fought off all overt and covert challenges to his presidency.

In 1981 I met Wynand Claassen for the first time since we played against each other in France in 1978. Wynand and another of the Springbok loose forwards, Burger Geldenhuys, played for Marmande that season and, as I recall it, we had a marvellous, flowing game against them. Now we met at the function after a test match for which he, as Springbok captain, had not been selected. His team had been beaten and an ingredient of that defeat had been its tactical impotence, no rush of inspiration to change pre-ordained strategy on the field.

Claassen's recall for the second test signalled a much more positive Springbok performance at Athletic Park — and a much less positive one by the All Blacks. One of the All Blacks featured in an event far from Athletic Park which precluded his presence in the test and thrust forward, not for the first time, the conservatism of the rugby administrators when confronted with a player's problem.

Gary Knight, clearly a key player in the All Black pack, was worried about new milking process on his Manawatu farm. There was some suggestion he might have to withdraw from the second test and this galvanised the local union into a rescue operation. Gary was offered an agricultural student when his need was for a man thoroughly experienced in dairying. He was not, of course, prepared to turn his herd over to inexperience for several days. He did not reveal the nature of

Wynand Claassen . . . his recall for the second test in 1981 sparked a more positive Springbok display.

his problem publicly. He said he was unavailable because he was tied to the farm of necessity.

That is known as amateurism. Presumably, had Gary been prepared to accept student help it would still have been known as amateurism. But had the New Zealand union worked through its many contacts to provide a seasoned man at seasoned pay that would have been professionalism. It is not the first time a farmer has been hogtied by the hidebound rules of rugby. Selector Peter Burke found the right sort of expert help so that Gary could play in the third test.

Wellington was an interesting place at the time of the second test. Not content with denying the Springboks use of their grounds to prepare, the Wellington City Council denied the All Blacks, too. The Mayor of Lower Hutt, Sir John Kennedy-Good, and his council were more accommodating, not to say more courageous and infinitely more courteous. To me it was irrelevant whether the council disagreed wth South Africa's politics. This was a Springbok rugby team, a gathering of individuals many of whom to my knowledge also disagreed with their country's system.

Assuming, as the media indicated, that the polls on the tour were indecisive, that New Zealand was evenly divided on the tour, the Wellington City Council, representing **all** the people of Wellington, had no right to make such a decision without going to the people of Wellington. It was not their right, given the circumstances of the electorate.

Some months later the Wellington mayor, Sir Michael Fowler, having decided it had been a most successful year for Wellington sportsmen, held a function to honour the occasion. High on the list of guests was the Wellington rugby team which had lifted the Ranfurly Shield from Auckland. I declined at first to attend because of my dissatisfaction with the council's attitude toward overseas visitors in my city the previous year. I am a parochial Wellingtonian, and I would defy even the mayor to measure his pride in Wellington against mine. But the council denied me, with my fellow-All Blacks, the use of the city's amenities. That was a pompous decision taken in some rosy glow of self-righteousness.

Feeling that strongly, then, I reviewed my decision not to attend the function. I should go and express my disapproval. It was the only straight thing to do. I asked a councillor to introduce me to the mayor, which she did. He was in a group of about four. I told Sir Michael I had intended to stay away as my own personal silent protest, but that as a Wellingtonian with a pioneering family background I had decided to protest against an action which had insulted me and which had smeared the city's reputation for dignified hospitality.

In the company of other councillors, he was obviously embarrassed and told me it had been a council decision upon which he had acted. I invited him to tell me he was not in favour of the decision and he declined to answer. I thanked him for inviting me to the function. Two councillors came to me and said they agreed entirely with my comments.

The following Saturday as captain of Wellington, I attended a Wellington radio station programme devoted to the Ranfurly Shield defence of the day against Hawkes Bay. The mayor was there. He was not at ease in my company. A couple of hours later we stood together nearby as thousands of fanatical supporters took part in a procession of floats. It was living proof of how much rugby meant to his city and mine. He was, in effect, recognising the public awareness of rugby and the benefit it was to Wellington. I said, "A great turnout, Mr Mayor." He agreed.

I recognise Sir Michael Fowler's many contributions to the advancement of Wellington. I am an admirer of his sketches of the city. But

I stand firmly on my resentment of the decision taken by him and his council in 1981.

For all its frustrations and all its trauma the 1981 season and the Springbok tour brought me my ultimate experience in rugby. The third test, for all its grotesque backdrop, was for me the summit.

There are emotional extremes in the careers of all sportsmen who play at the top level internationally for some years. In spite of the cynicism of that band of people who regard sport as self-indulgence without merit, representing one's country is a matter of intense pride, not in self but in country. I would nominate the third test against the 1981 Springboks as my most emotional high with the All Blacks. And unhesitatingly I offer you the Twickenham test against England in 1983 as the emotional low. The peak and the pits. One the total team effort in desperately difficult circumstances. One the incoherent, unplanned shambles. To relate the Eden Park experience to the Twickenham is to douse your strawberry pavlova with Famous Old-Fashioned Farmers Chutney.

There had been criticism through the years from my father and others that my approach to rugby was frivolous, especially my immediate approach to matches. I think that some might view my belated departure from the Okavango Swamps for the New Zealand trials in 1984 in that light. And there have been other hairline decisions which have seen me dicing with time to get back to New Zealand sufficiently early to convince selectors and public that I deserved any consideraion at all.

In the immediate preparation, the mental thing in dressing rooms and night-before concentration, I have found I have a switch in the mind. I switch on from the time I run on to the field. In dressing rooms I am, almost without exception, relaxed, having a surreptitious joke with Stu or Bernie or Hewie but not so as to intrude on those traditional pre-match meditations of other forwards. I know that some players need two or three days build-up to a big game. I do not. My application is to the task in hand and mostly that begins from the time I confront the opposition or at the time I go on to the training field or at the time I contribute to team-talks. It does not mean that I wrap myself in solemnity for days before the event.

But frivolous? No. I **know** myself. My commitment to the game is no less because my attitude in hotel or dressing room is not condemned cell material. It was not like that even before the third test against the Springboks but it was this match to which I turned myself with an almost desperate tenacity. This match had to be won for more reasons than any other test in which I had played — or have played since.

1981 — peak

Much has been made — and rightly so — of the stresses under which the Springboks played the 1981 series. Less has been made of the anxiety-stress under which the All Blacks played it. The Springboks were far from home and, frankly, that might have been to their advantage. The All Blacks' proximity to home and family placed upon them pressures of an emotional sort none of them had needed to handle before. Their homes, their wives, their children were under threat, whether mental or physical, from their own countrymen: abusive and obscene telephone calls, threats to destroy isolated farmhouses, threats of physical harm. New Zealand players were spat upon by New Zealanders, taunted, reviled.

The players' response had to be on the field. It became a matter of individual and team compulsion to win the third test. There must be no other result. To lose at Eden Park with the tests tied would have been a shattering emotional epxerience for every All Black in the team — substantially more so than for the Springboks for the very reasons I have given.

It was vital that the players lock out on the day the events which were extraneous to the actual playing of the game. That was not easy. We were told on the morning that explosives had been found in the grandstand. That was not designed to assist peace of mind. And, of course, there was awareness of the fanaticism of the protest-extremists and the intensity of confrontation there would be that day. Men are not robots. All the rugby motivation in the universe could not clear those shadows from the consciousness. And if there are still people in New Zealand who think the All Blacks shed from their minds and hearts everything except playing a game of rugby during that tour then

Zeroing in on the Springboks danger man Danie Gerber during the third test at Eden Park in 1985.

they do the players a grave injustice.

What emerged for me from that Saturday at Eden Park was the sort of satisfaction which can come only from being part of a team which is united in purpose, which feels bound together, man on man, with no deviation from commitment to the goal. It was a total experience in the idealism of "team".

Yet "team" was at the heart of a pre-match concern for me. Within one rugby team there are a number of "teams". New Zealand places great faith in its loose-forward team . . . Mourie, Shaw, Mexted; Stewart, Shaw, Mexted. There was familiarity in both. But Shelford, Old, Mexted? How to box-up a loose-forward team performance, a lineout compatability with two players new to international rugby, one of them playing out of position, in a test match of unprecedented pressures?

Graham Mourie refused to play the Springboks on personal principle. Mark Shaw and Kenny Stewart had played in the first two tests. Now Shaw was out with injury and Stewart had been made the undeserved scapegoat for a listless forward performance in the second.

Geoff Old, my touring partner of 1980, was a sometime number eight-sometime lock with Manawatu and a fine, committed player in provincial rugby. Now he was to go into this test as the blindside flanker. Frank Shelford had impressed everyone with a dynamic performance for the New Zealand Maoris against the Springboks. But for the first time I would be playing with two flankers I had never played with — and in the most important match of my life. We could hardly be labelled "combination" and a loose-forward combination is a crucial element in rugby, particularly in the circumstances of this game where we were playing a team of awesome size and power with a very dangerous kicker at fly-half and strength on the wings. If ever we needed a loose-forward unit this was it.

I was bloody worried. More worried than I had ever been approaching a test. Suddenly I had become the senior-pro by default. How would Geoff and I work at 6 and 7 in the lineouts? What about the cover-jump on the low throw? How would Frank and I work in the close-contact pressure phases where understanding was vital?

Geoff played with some sort of divine inspiration, magnificent in every way. He gave us extra strength in the lineout where we could alternate with throws to either 6 or 7. How on earth the New Zealand Rugby Union expected me to mark him in a national championship match at Athletic Park the day after I'll never know. Frank was furiously committed to the tight-loose game which developed. The lack of practised combination did not appear to affect the match, due probably to the Springbok pattern which emphasised kicking rather than running. Twice Frank recovered second phase ball to feed me — again the Mourie pattern. At the end of the day I was proud that we three had been able spontaneously to form an effective combination from an unlikely beginning.

Throughout the game I was unaware of the turmoil with phosphorous bombs, detonations, flares, flour bombs. After the game when someone said an aircraft had blitzed the ground continuously, making 57 passes, some of them crazily low, I did not believe it. Obviously, there were occasions when it was there. The flour bag which hit Gary Knight was not your ordinary Monty Python flying flour-bag. But the concentration on the game was such that what I was later to see on film I found unbelievable.

First test v Springboks, 1981. Tackled by Eben Jansen minutes after he had kicked me in the face. Kenny Stewart's characteristic commitment comes through clearly.

No doubt the Springboks felt as strongly as we the need to show in the final test that all had not been in vain. They had been subjected to contempt in their host country; they came from a land whose political philosophy was under broad international criticism. The feeling in both camps, then, made it inevitable that Eden Park would be the arena for a titanic power struggle. There was desperation here, in both sides.

The close feeling of the All Blacks was the first emotional tug I had. I knew this was no three-on-three loose forward contest and to the winners of that battle, the spoils. This had the feel of eight-on-eight and to the winner of that, the winning of the game. It is one of the great old cliches of rugby, of course, that no match is won before it is won up front. Both teams, perhaps as never before in a test match between the countries, went into this sharply conscious of the truth of it.

From the first All Black forward surge under a Dave Loveridge kick I had that indescribable rush of confidence when you sense you are part of a domineering All Black pack. With no disrespect to the backs I say that in this match the old cliche held good. In the purely selfish sense, I was elated with the loose forwards and pleased with my own contribution to the game. I knew I was getting to the ball in the loose, defensively and attacking, that where the play was, so was I. That is the secret of contentment for a loose forward: that he is where the action is, whether making his tackles or playing his part in distribution.

There were feats of greatness among the front five. Gary Whetton, a boy, designated to mark Louis Moolman, one of the finest lineout forwards South Africa had produced, did so well that you knew he would lock many All Black scrums. In terms of his lack of maturity and experience Whetton's performance that day was one of the most astonishing of my time in rugby.

The All Blacks manufactured the two tries we scored — one a Hewson-Wilson inspiration and the other by Gary Knight immediately after I had thought I had it. I had actually crossed the line, down low driving, but as I crashed to ground the ball somehow jammed against Danie Gerber's knee. I was able to control the pop-back. Shelford went over the top and Loveridge got knocked off as he went for it. Then, on the other side of the ruck, Gary was unstoppable.

The Springboks scored their three through Ray Mordt on the right wing. There were elements of their opportunism and of looseness in our concentration on the ball on the ground and in the air for two of those tries and the other resulted directly from ball spilled by the

Springbok winger Ray Mordt slices inside Steven Pokere at Eden Park. He scored three tries in the explosive third test.

South Africans in a Lachie Cameron tackle. Tries are tries, of course. But we felt the frustration of seeing a 16-3 half-time lead being blown wide apart by rub of the green more than tries constructed through plan and efficiency.

When Naas Botha placed the ball for the conversion which would have given South Africa the lead and probably the match I said to Andy Haden, "If he kicks this there's absolutely no justice in the world." Andy nodded. The kick missed yet I felt no elation. The scoreline stood at 22-22 and to me that was neither good enough nor fair enough. There was time, but everything seemed to be moving at a crazy pace toward a final whistle. My own feelings were of desperate urgency but never of futility.

When Allan Hewson took that final kick at goal I knew it would go over. It seemed right that it should. The Agen in me took over for an instant of abandonment. But the game went on. Now Clive Norling was the danger man — not Mordt, not Botha. Whistle. Oh hell, what's **this** one for? He had us scared rigid. During the match everyone, including the Springboks, was on edge when the whistle went. Now with the seconds at their last gasp Norling's self-appointed star-status had us over the edge.

But that's the way it ended. Everyone had played himself into exhaustion but there was no pain. Now came the appraisals. The Springboks deserved a draw at least? You had to be out there playing to know they didn't. Some of the long-distance appraisals had snipes at Hewson for failing to be more positive on Mordt's advances yet generally there was understatement of the degree of difficulty of his penalty goal to win the match. Positionally, for Hewie no problem. But with the match at crisis point, an extremely difficult kick.

I am one of those whose approach to a game is sometimes influenced by Hewie. For a number eight with a clear recognition of where, in every normal circumstance, he should be, it can be a bit of a frustration playing with him. But I would never have been without him. It is a coach's triumph to stimulate the confidence of a player like Hewie, to encourage him to express his strengths and his talents. If Ian Upston had not been the Wellington coach at the right time we may never have had an Allan Hewson, All Black.

We have had outstanding all-round players at fullback in Wellington, notably Clive Currie and Brian Cederwall, but none with the freakish skills of Hewson. He was so very calm, one of the most in-control footballers I have played with and that was an integral part of his matchless skill.

The modifications I have had to bring to my own game playing with Hewie are of minimal consequence compared with the delight his gifts have brought to rugby. By that I mean my sharpened awareness when the opposition puts the ball in the air; where I prefer to run across the advantage line in our own territory in case of midfield breakdown, I run five or six yards deeper so that if the ball is in the air I am in a position to catch or recover it . . .

In some matches, depending on the opposition, that deeper running had been intentional. With Hewie it became a sub-conscious tactic. It meant I was further from the ball if there was a breakdown on the advantage line and the flanker was there looking for support. And in the tests against South Africa there was frustration in reverting to the old corner-flagging routine. In the second test at Athletic Park I found myself roaring behind the backline when we lost the ball in set phases, to endeavour to tackle someone before the corner-flag. Germishuys had scored one try by a simple overlap and two or three minutes later threatened to do the same again and I was able to knock him into touch at the corner.

But without Hewie would we have scored that beautifully sensitive try through Stu Wilson in the third test? Not possible. Would another have kicked the goal to win? Doubtful. Allan Hewson was a rare artist in New Zealand rugby. Consider that before exaggerating his faults.

1983 — pits

When your head is jammed between the substantial bums of a couple of sweaty locks, your ears are stinging and the sweat is getting into a laceration on your face and it's raining you usually accept it as part of the deal. Even in training. But on this occasion I thought, "Just what the hell am I doing here?" Unhealthy symptoms. At least I didn't ask what the hell we were all doing there, though I was tempted.

It was one of those drizzly, drifty days out of London. A training session by the All Blacks of 1983. It was a jacked-up tour to replace the planned one to Argentina where a war of sorts had made absentee New Zealanders personae non grata because, I think, from our vast arsenal of sophisticated weaponry we had offered the ill-equipped British a frigate. Argentina would have been excitement. Argentina would have seduced every senior All Black to tour. Scotland-England had switched them off in droves. I can't say we expected hard times because in spite of the absence of players like Gary Knight, John Ashworth, Andy Dalton, Gary Whetton, Andy Haden, Graeme Higginson, Dave Loveridge, Allan Hewson we had the built-in capacity to win both tests. But I can say we deserved hard times because we failed intelligently to plan the defeat of England, we had no capacity on the field to "feel" the game and change strategy accordingly because there was no on-field communication between forwards and skipper out on the wing. When the tour started going ragged at the edges there was no confident stitching and sewing to tidy it up.

It was a tour managed with little understanding of players' difficulties and needs and it was a tour coached by one of the finest gentlemen in rugby but one who could not come to grips with the require-

Ollie Campbell . . . the only 1983 British Lion who concerned the All Blacks.

Bryce Rope . . . indulged a whim by appointing a winger as tour captain.

ments as circumstances turned the tour sour. Stu Wilson was as fine a captain off the field as you could desire in Andy Dalton's absence. But coach Bryce Rope really indulged a whim by appointing a wing as his touring captain and his indulgence was punished. The manager, Paul Mitchell, failed to win the confidence of the players and on a tour with so many new All Blacks this was a significant blow to its chances of success.

Bum 1 that day as we trained for the match against Midlands belonged to Albert Anderson. Bum 2 belonged to Geoff Old. We had just been to Twickenham where we had beaten London Division in a characterless match in which a Scottish referee named Eric Allen practised diligently for his All-Britain whistling championship final against Roger Whittaker. On the strength of his dress-rehearsal I'm sure he bolted in.

Now we were heading for defeat by Midlands, an uneven draw against Scotland (a match we commanded but gave half away through indiscipline) and the grand tour finale against England, the test from which New Zealand rugby took nothing, and least of all pride . . .

So what had happened since the soaring pride of 1981 at Eden Park? We had tasted rugby in Romania. Hard men the Romanians, much infatuated, though, with the kicking game. I hope the political pressures which have squeezed the gaiety out of life in a beautiful country have not forever squeezed the Romanian rugby game dry of Latin in-

Parc des Princes, Paris, 1981 — the "front throw" works perfectly against the best, Jean-Luc at right.

On tour, France '81 . . . Malcolm Hood, physio, Geoff Old under his arm, Doug Rollerson, Arthur Stone, Paul Koteka, Bernie Fraser, Andy Haden.

ventiveness and charm. We had toured France, a patchy tour which came together only in the second and last test at Parc des Princes when we comprehensively dismantled the French. That was a specially satisfying performance by a New Zealand team which had been scratching for organisation and which, for some of its matches against French Selections, had taken a media-beating. We had an inspiring plea from Mourie before the test and we went into it with fierce determination and a game plan which, adhered to, wrote off the French forwards and with that destroyed the confidence of the backs.

The Wallabies in 1982 came back from a beating at Christchurch to squeeze us out at Wellington and then took a walloping a Eden Park. Eden Park . . . it has been a good ground for me and for the All Blacks of my time, big-scoring bonanzas for rugby: 40-15 against Scotland, 25-22 against South Africa, 33-18 against Australia, 38-6 against British Isles, 31-18 against France.

That 38-6 result against the British Isles might indicate that we could have taken any old team on the Scotland-England tour and succeeded. But that was a Lions team without teeth. It has been suggested that such a big win in a game the All Blacks dominated everywhere must have brought satisfaction comparable to the defeat of the Springboks two years earlier. But it was not so. Satisfaction comes from placing fitness, skill, commitment, team-work on the line against opponents who are going to force you to expend every ounce of those things. The

Jean-Luc Joinel goes! Note the French backline in support alignment. Eden Park, 1984.

Eden Park, 1984 — which way's the goalline?

I'll never forget this game — and not for the barbed wire and the bombs. For me this was the ultimate rugby match. South Africa, Eden Park, 1981.

Marking my great French rival Jean-Luc Joinel during the second test at Eden Park in 1984.

A great game for rugby . . . our first official test against Argentina, Buenos Aires, 1985, and the beginning of what is sure to be a strong relationship.

Tireless Cowboy Shaw delivers juicy possession to Andrew Donald — against Northern Division at Gateshead in 1983, a game we won 27-21.

1983.

If you can't decipher the signature the artist of this delightful caricature is Wynand Claassen, captain of the 1981 Springboks and my Natal team mate.

Latin passion . . . a magnificent crowd, the Argentines, and they created a true test atmosphere at Buenos Aires, 1985, first test.

England suffer the most typical of all New Zealand forward procedures
individual power so closely supported that it becomes a unified surge.

Springboks did that. The Lions of 1983 did not.

Taking that team, I can lift from it only Ollie Campbell as an individual who demanded All Black planning. Our aim was to cancel Ollie as the linch-pin of the backs and to so discipline ourselves that he could not kick the Lions into victory. He faced the same sort of pressures in the provincial games and I doubt that his team-mates understood what this meant in physical and mental stress. Ollie had the capacity to call the tune in a match whether by kicking, running or in an area of rugby not many fly-halves consider their duty lies: Ollie loved tackling. He would make as many tackles in a game as you would expect from a loose forward and he would thrive on that contact-rugby. He is a delightful, sincere man. I last saw him in Dublin early in 1984, on a spoofers' rugby weekend to watch Ireland play Wales. Ollie had an agonising game outside an indecisive scrum-half and Wales took charge of the game. On Sunday he came to the airport to see me off and we had a farewell spoof for morning tea. Ollie had his only victory of the weekend.

Between 1981 and the Scotland-England tour, then, we had played 11 tests, 10 of which we had won. The wheels fell off with the cancellation of the Argentina tour. The only established test forwards who declared themselves available for Scotland-England were Mark Shaw and myself. I was there because I saw it as a duty to be there, that in a tour team populated by new players there would be something substantial for me to contribute. But as the tour unfolded I found my contribution other than on the field was not required. I felt — and **was** — suppressed, never called on as one who had the means to communicate with young players.

There was a great deal of conjecture about the inner-working of the 1983 tour. Cowboy Shaw, having been made pack-leader, was said to be at logger-heads with me . . . at each other's throats, these two, wrote one Sunday newspaper reporter from a distance of 12,000 miles. Cowboy and I couldn't believe that shit-stirring of that sort would get any credibility but we found people actually believed it. We had no fight. We have been good friends for a long time. There were a number of things about that tour I disagreed with and Cowboy was aware of this — and, I think, shared some of my concerns. But they did not include confrontations with him or ill-feeling toward him.

It has been stated by Stu Wilson himself, in the book he produced with Bernie Fraser, that he should not have been captain of the team. Stu said he found the position frustrating to the point where he himself was in a turmoil psychologically, and that he had little understanding

History in Bucharest . . . New Zealand's first test match in Romania, my first, and only, retirement from a test match . . . popped rib, Malcolm Hood in attendance.

from Paul Mitchell. As a field captain Stu was simply too far removed from the action out there on the wing. Here was a team with three new locks, a new hooker, four new props. Neither half-back had played a test, neither fullback had played a test, nor had one of the wings and a utility back.

Stu has written that I should have been captain of the 1983 All Blacks.

I will say that in the makeup of that team there were only two possibilities — Mark Shaw and myself. I do understand Bryce Rope did not want me because he saw me as a threat to his style. And I must say there have been a couple of occasions when I have rather abruptly indicated my dissent from his notions on loose forward play. I guess I must have cancelled myself out. If that was so then Bryce had no other option but to go for Cowboy. In appointing Stu he was playing some private little side-game. It became clear the team had to be led by someone who could **feel** what was happening up front. In the forwards you **feel** the way the game is turning, whether you have ascendancy, whether there is co-ordinated opposition, whether they are coming back at you. The scrum-half or, perhaps, the first five-eighths may **feel** it but from further out than that it is hopeful assessment, not **feel**.

It was **feel** and urgent action on it which was demanded in the test at Twickenham. We had played and lost to Midlands. Led by Peter Wheeler, Midlands devised a tactic to destroy our drive. As soon as we mounted a drive from set or broken play the tactic was to pull the front man to ground thereby collapsing the maul. They were prepared to let us drive, to give ground so that they could stop play in this way knowing that if we then won the ball it would be slow and of little use.

Peter Wheeler was to captain England. Having achieved startling success at Leicester with that tactic it was worth ten quid on the nose that he would do it again at Twickenham. Stu anticipated that clearly. On two occasions I suggested we should continue to drive but modify it slightly by moving the ball away from the collapsible area, by moving it deeper in the maul — but, above all, let us continue to drive. English teams hate this. But what Bryce contrived when it came to the England match was to abandon our drive altogether and attempt to strike from first phase ball at all times, moving it from a stationary position as quickly as possible and we would be first to the breakdown. Not bad. But . . .

Imagine rugged old campaigners like Maurice Colclough, Wheeler himself, Colin White and a real contestant like Steve Bainbridge realising the All Blacks, of all people, rather than modify their driving technique had decided not to drive at all. The thing went full cycle. These All Black forwards were not to be feared — so England drove it at us. Rugby is very psychological in the forward confrontation and for many years we have been dominating English packs, so much so that they play in awe of us. But here, they sensed very early we were not the overpowering combination and they became first confident and then arrogant.

There had been signs in the early part of the game that we would play good tight-knit stuff and, in fact, we were looking good. But it evaporated. At the end of it Albert Anderson, Gary Braid, Brian McGrattan and myself had won a substantial share of the lineout possession but we had, as a pack, done nothing to commit the English forwards to quench our drive. We let them loose on our ball.

After Maurice Colclough scored his try on a forward drive I said to Stu, "We've got to have these bastards on. These guys are dealing to us. To **us**! We've got to turn it around." As it happened we nearly pulled it off with a "try" by Craig Green — six inches short of the posts. But the damage had been done long since.

At the end of it I felt as low as ever I have. We hadn't been beaten at Twickenham since Prince Obolensky scored that fabulous try in 1935. We had failed to plan for the obvious and when it came to the crunch we did not switch tactics when the state of the game screamed for it. I know, too, how Stu Wilson felt when it was finished. He had done so well maintaining morale in a raw touring team but what he wanted most was success on the field.

I hope this tour hammered home to the New Zealand Rugby Union that management on tour must be in the hands of a man who is constantly aware of the players' difficulties, who thinks of them and cares about them. The Dick Littlejohns and Ray Harpers have the touch and Russ Thomas was esteemed for his efficiency and as a great image-maker for New Zealand.

No All Black on tour should ever hear this again: "Expenses are a bit of a problem. I just haven't had time to do them. I have had a very busy itinerary. I haven't just been sitting down while you chaps have been sleeping, you know." A manager cannot merely **expect** the respect of the players. Unless he is prepared to earn it by being a players' manager he will receive something very considerably less. On a tour as difficult as this one with all its new players the captain has duties enough without having also to cope with passed-on management jobs.

The peak and the pits . . . New Zealand 25, South Africa 22, Eden Park, September 12, 1981; England 15, New Zealand 9, Twickenham, November 19, 1983.

But even 1983 had compensations if you were prepared to take a hand on your own behalf. I had a yen to participate in the National Spoofing Championships in London the night before the game against London Division. I was not to play in it because I had six stitches in a gash over the eye from the previous match against Northern Division. But it would have been jolly unseemly, I thought, to be observed leav-

England, 1983 . . . "Stu, we've got to have a crack at these guys up front."

ing our London hotel for a night out in these circumstances. My room was on the fourth floor of St Ermin's Hotel. I was in white tie and tails. How was I to negotiate four floors and escape the hotel through the kitchen unobserved? An accomplice? Of course. Bernard Gabriel Fraser, man of many parts and always good for a sneaky adventure or two.

So Bernie, over-acting like hell, crept through the hotel corridors and down the flights of stairs ahead of me. It was Academy Award stuff, each floor and each flight negotiated with great hushing and vast pretence of 007 connections round every corner. Bernie made the kitchen, tripped over a couple of phantom corpses, shushed me fiercely, and gestured grandly to the kitchen exit. Then Bernie, bless him, disappeared. I went out the door. It clicked shut behind me.

I was underground. Street level somewhere up there and inaccessible. It was pitch black and cold. So cold. I felt around and found the bottom rung of a fire-escape. Anything would do as long as it was up. So I stretched up to the first step and, like a thrust from an icicle, cold air shafted into my backside. Split pants we call it in the business. I carried on regardless with absolutely no idea of my geography. A window, **any** window . . . **please** let there be a window unlocked. I scrabbled at anonymous window frames risking identification as a peeping-tom at best and a mad rapist at worst, finally found one open, slid through it like silk, darted across someone's room and out into a corridor.

No Bernie. Boldness be my friend. I stalked through the hotel and found my way to the parking lot and from there it was a breeze. Played in the spoofing champs at The Rugby Club by courtesy mine host Jeff Butterfield, former England and Lions centre, but played like a drop-out from an arithmetic class for the retarded. There were 50 spoofers from all over Britain plus an Australian and four New Zealanders (including Brett Codlin) resident in Britain. After spoofing, a long night at Toppers and at 5am a re-entry to the hotel which was about as furtive as the grand march from Aida.

Mission accomplished, no harm done, tour frustration eased approximately 200 per cent.

Working out the Boks

"Life," said Mr Bill Endicott, "is not a rehearsal." Only a spoofer could have said it as meaningfully across thousands of miles of Indian Ocean, the Australian continent, the Tasman Sea and into the Mexted telephone in Tawa. Just another spoofers' cliche but delivered with such studied pomposity that each time it was said it was like a gem of spontaneous oratory inspired by the company. What Mr Endicott was saying from Johannesburg was that I should hot-foot to South Africa in 1982 and play a season of rugby. Just on the spur of the moment I couldn't come up with any good reason why I shouldn't.

Mr Endicott was of the opinion, he said, that this would be one of life's great adventures . . . "Mr Mexted, consider this well, I implore you." So, having considered it well for several seconds, I agreed. I spoke to him of climate, the need I felt to be living beside a beach. He noted, with authority, that this probably would cancel out Johannesburg which, being at an altitude of 1753 metres, had lamentably few surfing beaches. So he offered Cape Town as being rather like New Zealand or Durban which had summer all year round. Exit Mr Endicott, enter Wynand Claassen of Durban Collegians and captain of Natal.

Nothing, said Wynand, will be a problem. Figuratively, he was saying "state your price" — but only in terms of fares and what sort of work I would care to have. What sort of overpaid work. That had a familiar ring to it as Wynand knew it would, he having done his stint in France too. But the thing Wynand offered beyond all else was the opportunity to play number eight. That, for the Springbok captain and a specialist in the position himself, was a generous gesture. As it eventuated we found that the right mix over there was Wynand at number eight, myself on the open-side flank and at seven in the lineout and Craig Ross, Bay of Plenty, at the blindside flank and at six in the lineout. Craig Ross in South Africa was a magnificent tight-loose forward and, with Mark Shaw, the best lineout six I have played with.

It is vital in the seven jumping position to have a six who will give me the room to jump, to provide space between my opponent and me. All I ask is that I have that room to move and that the only person I have to beat is my direct opposite. A specialised segment of my lineout work is on the low-throw and as a cover-jumper. I originated that throw to seven by accident and now a lot of us use it — Geoff Old, Alan Whetton and a number of the "new-style" number eights. It started when I was playing both my club and representative rugby with Brendan Gard'ner. It started with me cover-jumping him and it became such an effective operation that I started using it, too. The further back in the lineout the throw is coming the more difficult to win clean ball — more time for obstruction, more spread for inaccuracy in the throw to take effect, more time for every other interfering bludger to have a go at the ball. So the "low one" became my surprise ball.

Playing with Natal was more than just a floating phase, a passing experience. It was being part of a crusade with Wynand up there at the front carrying the banner. He had gone to Natal from Northern Transvaal in 1980 which was a bit like swapping a strait-jacket for a floral caftan. Wynand had felt so frustrated locked into Northern's traditional graunch-game — the massive pack delivering ball for the fly-half to kick for position and then for goal — that he sought the freedom of the flowing Natal game and set out to show it could be successful. For this season, Natal had been relegated to the Currie Cup B division and he was committed to getting it back up into the Cup play-offs.

At the beginning of the season we played Orange Free State in the first of three matches to celebrate the opening of the new Ellis Park. It was spectacular. Not just this great stadium, but the rugby we played in that game against a first division province, was inspirational stuff. In my first experience of playing rugby at extreme altitude I understood why touring teams are so fastidious about the right mix in their itinerary; the heaving for breath, the light-headedness, the searing of the throat. And going into the first lineout I looked at my opponent and he was two inches taller and two stone heavier than me. Then I saw Craig Ross turning to look at me with his eyebrows up on his hairline. I looked at his man. Two inches taller and two stone heavier. I looked at Wynand and he was still measuring his guy. We three, to most standards, were a very big loose forward trio. Over there they have battalions of giant young loose forwards. They breed these mammoth players and turn them loose on the little kids from Natal.

Natal came away from Free State in the second spell to win by about 20 points and Craig Ross became the first New Zealander to score a try on new Ellis Park — and a hell of a try it was. Wynand and I handled twice and Craig outsped the cover over 35 yards. When the cheering subsided, a renowned spoofer, Mr. Simon Rumney, stood in the crowd and announced with exaggerated pride: "In New Zealand I slept on that man's floor!" And sat down again. From everything I saw of Ross I was surprised he had not been talent-scouted more astutely at home. He was very much the big, fast tight-flanker New Zealand teams specialise in and though Bay of Plenty used him often as a lock that should not have hidden his worth in his specialist position.

Life in Durban, you will understand, was not all rugby. The beach was my life, too, and I made time to get away to Jeffreys Bay and the supertubes. I'm sure a lot of Afrikaners saw me as some sort of of casual gypsy, for their liking too much given to the sea and the social life. There was the time I was invited to play in an invitation XV and went directly to the assembly from Jeffreys Bay, still dripping salt water. My room-mate, Schalk Burger, an earnest young man destined to be a test player in 1984, studied me with more than passing suspicion, an attitude I hope was re-assessed during the game.

Had I not played well they would never have taken me seriously again, the only overseas player in the team and a surfie to boot. But given the nature of the match I decided to run the ball at every chance and it paid off in gold. I could see this tall young guy in our team, familiar somehow, and I remembered watching him play for Pretoria Harlequins. Jannie Breedt, 6ft 5, 15½ stone, flanker, and he liked to run but just lacked a touch of confidence. I grabbed him and said, "Have a crack, Jannie. These blokes hate it when big, fast guys run at them with the ball." So he did and between us we had a ball. Jannie was still only 21 and I thought, come 1985 he will be trouble for us. Except that probably they wouldn't pick him. And that same mentality probably dictated Rob Louw's in-out career with the Springboks.

They're bad selectors, the South Africans. While success in the provincial championships is based on the power game without broad vision that is the game which will be perpetuated at all levels. Anyone with flair is regarded with some misgivings, seen to be a bit of a showman. Knock that out of them at all costs, they reckon, and you might find a good Springbok forward underneath. So rather than Jannie Breedt they would go for a big Boer crewcut who eats three raw steaks for breakfast and does as he's told. They don't look for the bonus skills. They look for the basic.

Without tours from other International Rugby Board countries the South African game is in a state of perpetual motion, players switching provinces all over the place. Musical chairs, and they're playing it even on the very eve of important matches. There's no pretence about it. Where the money is the players go and if it's not money up front it's money in houses or in some other sort of material form. It was that sort of transaction which brought Ockie Oosthuizen out of retirement. Ockie was seen as an outstanding success on the 1981 Springbok tour here and his early retirement sent shockwaves through the rugby system. But, with due respect to Ockie as an industrious prop, our front row in those tests just didn't rate the Springboks at all. The only prop they considered a difficult opponent was Hempies du Toit, the Stellenbosch wine-maker. A hard man, Hempies, even if he does grow chrysanthemums as a sideline.

Ockie was snapped up by Randberg, a new club which set out to buy itself senior status in as short a time as possible. I know of other players bought in to clubs and provinces by straight cash inducement, maybe by a wealthy club supporter whose only return other than the advancement of the club would be to have the player along to business luncheons and social events as an ego-booster.

Anyway, Natal prospered much as Wynand hoped it would. There were downers, of course, such as the match three of us believed we could win. That was the main reason we lost. The other 12 did not believe we could win and their whole demeanour in the changing room showed it. It was a pall of depression, induced by this almost pathological fear some provinces have when they are to play the Blue Bulls, Northern Transvaal. Craig Ross, Wynand and myself wanted to climb into the Northerns, take the game to them, but the hearts of the rest of the boys were not in it. I have never experienced this in New Zealand. I have never played with or against a team which expected so deeply it would lose that it tossed in the towel before the game began. Even when the East Coast goes to Canterbury or Buller to Auckland there's a will to win.

As it was, the loose forward team came out of the match well and other than our positive moral approach to it we might least have expected to perform at peak on the paddock. We had played Boland at Wellington on the Saturday — nostalgia here, with Wellington so reminiscent of Wellington at home on a breezy, damp day and the Boland players in black with gold trim. We won narrowly and Wynand

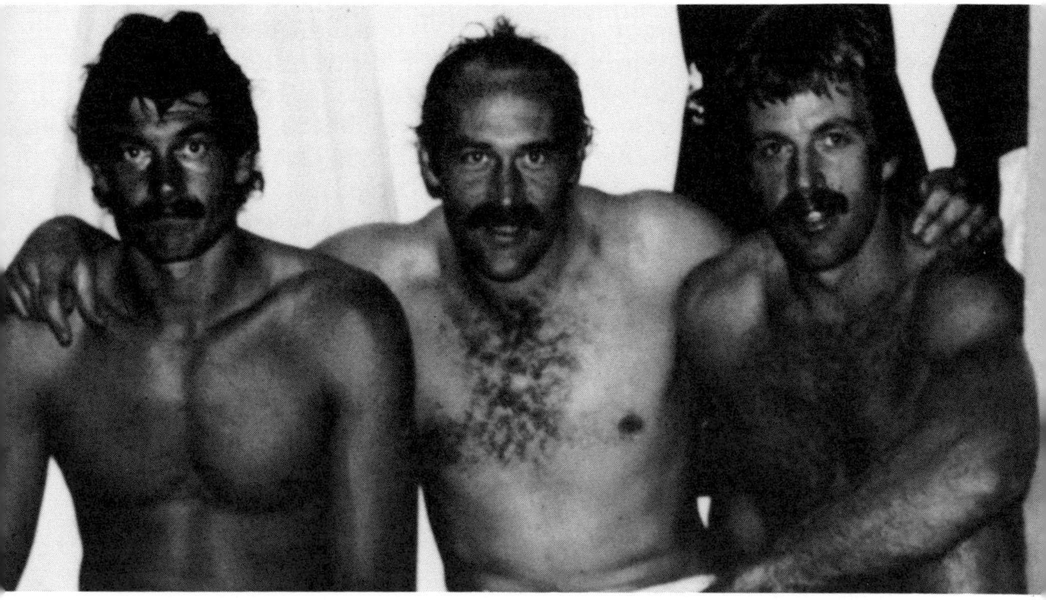

First match at Ellis Park, Johannesburg, 1982, with Wynand Claassen and kiwi Craig Ross, Natal v Orange Free State — a highly effective loose forward team.

decided it would be good for the two New Zealanders to relax for a couple of days in the Cape. So he took us to Hempies du Toit's vineyard and Hempies introduced us to his premier wine, Alto Rouge. Having introduced us to it, he reintroduced us to it immediately and so the treadmill rolled. Alto Rouge is a greatly sought-after wine and we came to the considered opinion after spending a couple of days in its company that its reputation was richly deserved.

We got back to Durban in time for Tuesday training, the day before the match against Northern Transvaal. I suppose that added fuel to the criticism which, Wynand wrote in his book, went on in whispers about my approach to the game. Sometimes I surfed the morning of a club match but always aware I had a match to play — and really just frolicking. My rugby was never affected by my lifestyle because, just as in New Zealand, I was able to switch on to the task in hand, mentally and physically. I was aware there was a fair bit of chipping at me when I took off to play the centennial match in Parma, Italy, but so there was when I said it was time to return to New Zealand to try to qualify for the All Blacks to play the Wallabies. Some people actually believed I should have stayed — that my duty was more to Natal than to New Zealand.

It was extraordinary, but rather typified for me the disturbing lack of concern in South Africa for what had happened to New Zealand during the 1981 tour. If they had any conception of the appalling events of that year it rarely showed. I found it very difficult to accept that what New Zealand had been through could be so casually dismissed. It was as if South Africans had deliberately locked it out of their consciousness. Thinking people like Wynand Claassen were still shocked by it. Wynand said that before South Africa accepted any tour anywhere it must more seriously consider the consequences to the host country. But the blanket mentality had dismissed the New Zealand experience as something which had happened to someone else.

One of Natal's favourite sons is the old Springbok number eight Tommy Bedford who once criticised the Springbok selectors for their lack of attention to the province and related their indifference to Natal being the last bastion of the British Empire in South Africa. When I spoke at a club luncheon in Pietermaritzburg they raised the Union Jack before the show got under way. Some of their British ways are more British than the British. My club persisted with men-only bars and it was my attitude to this which, no doubt, further irritated the traditionalists in the club. I am not opposed to tradition. In respect for great things past I am an ardent traditionalist. But there are some customs eagerly labelled "traditional" which are really just old-fashioned, a stodgy — even boorish — clinging to old ways in a new world. Men-only bars come into that category.

Early in my stay in Durban the club had a pre-season match followed by the inevitable South African barbecue — a braaivleis. It was such a relaxed show that I entered the bar in shorts and jandals. Club members were not impressed. But when they saw the girl by my side it was like one of those old English newspaper cartoons, "The man who . . ." I was the man who took a young woman into the High School Old Boys' men-only bar. All those shocked, infuriated, dumbfounded looks. One of the old-timers came to me and said, "This is beyond the pale. Get out of this bar." I noticed that everyone was wearing reefers, white shirts, ties and even shoes and socks. I was aware I should not have taken the girl in there but that was a deliberate flouting of what I saw as an archaic rule. But I had not been aware of the strict dress discipline in 30 degree heat with 100 per cent humidity. So the old chap was livid. "Are you really asking me to leave?" I asked. He assured me he was. So I left with my girl and my jandals after telling him I'd never go into the bar again. And I didn't. Not till a year later.

When I went back for the next season to play only club rugby I had

The Bok front row of 1981, 20-stone Flippie van der Merwe (left), Willie Kahts and Ockie Oosthuizen . . . not a combination we feared.

a call from a club administrator inviting me to join him for a drink. Where? In the club bar. No way . . . "It's all right you silly bugger, you've won. It's open to ladies now." A triumph, and not really so hard-won either. I found I enjoyed the atmosphere and the company in the open-air social pavilion more, anyway. And it was there that a gravelly-voiced Australian sang and played the piano standing up, lying down, on his head and sometimes, but rarely, sitting down. His name was Dick Cocks. He had toured South Africa with the Wallabies in 1969, stayed on and become an entertainment legend in Durban.

I had congenial employment in Durban as sales promotions manager with McCarthy Sigma and it was through my close working relationship with black and Indian that I came more clearly to understand the complexities of bringing the races together. With the blacks it is a case of nations which from the beginning of their time have been enemies. Now **there** is tradition. In the motor company the Zulus and the Xhosas had to work separately, to have separate toilet facilities. If they came into contact they fought, not just fist-fights to stop at the first sight of blood, but terrible maiming brawls which, if not halted, would have ended in death.

There is little understanding in New Zealand of the deep hatred with which one black nation regards another. We are inclined to talk here of a great black uprising, of the need for the black people to have equal status in all things including the administration of the country. The battle within that battle would be to have Zulu working with Xhosa or Zulu working with his bitter but related enemy, the Pondo. The recent battles between Zulu and Pondo and Zulu and Xhosa may have done something to bring home to New Zealanders the profundity of this historical enmity between black nations but I doubt that the significance of it projected into a one-man one-vote future has registered. There are many aspects of the South African political system which cannot be upheld. Apartheid in its worst expressions and administered by the hard-line high-veldt Boer is an appalling system. The archetypal Afrikaner is arrogant, bombastic, narrow-minded. He is also hard-working, proud and convinced that what he has made of South Africa should not now be taken from him. That is what he sees as the inevitable result of reversal of the homeland policy and the introduction of a one-man one-vote system virtually overnight.

Many black people foresee the problems, too. Many seek a system through which the power to vote would be won by educational attainment through a schooling system into which vastly more of the nation's wealth was poured.

Because I went to play rugby in South Africa and to surf there and live part of my life there I have been put down as an apologist for the system. Tell that to the thousands upon thousands of tourists who nominate South Africa as their place for a holiday or to the international businessmen who ply their trade with South Africa. At least I have **learned** something of South Africa. At least I can criticise from the advantage of having observed. At least I can understand that measures which have been taken to dismantle some of apartheid's more reprehensible laws and which have been written off here as sham or cosmetic are in fact giant steps considering how deeply embedded the laws had become in the Afrikaner psyche.

I admire the approach to self-education of David Kirk, the All Black half-back who went on a hitch-hiking expedition to southern Africa in 1984. I met him there, having played with him in the 1983 All Black trial. I had missed the North-South match at Wanganui in 1982 when he was a key part of South's upset win over North and I had heard that he had a keen mind for the game as well as physical quickness and courage. It was clear from the trial we played that he would quickly challenge for an All Black position. He wanted to see South Africa for himself, to judge for himself, possibly because he wanted to be able to stand off with a clear mind when the time came for decision-making in 1985.

Of course there is unrest and dissatisfaction in the over-populated townships and it is an environment tailor-made for political pressure from the direction South Africa most fears — communism. It is increasingly clear from film of township unrest that the banner of the hammer and sickle has become high-fashion. There is no need for reds-under-the-beds fiction. It is now accepted the influence is in there while white and black South Africans are fighting Cubans on the Namibian border.

Where New Zealanders finish their rugby training session with a couple of beers and talk about rugby or cricket or last night's party South Africans sit around and talk about new armaments. They do their three years' straight service and go back six weeks a year on the border. Sometimes they don't come back to play rugby.

South Africa's wealth is coveted and so is its strategic position. It produces a huge percentage of the free world's gold, diamonds, uranium, and a vast array of metallic and non-metallic minerals

There is a great deal of selective morality in attitudes to South Africa — much of it based on the fact that racism is written into the country's legislation. Of course it is reprehensible and to point to the savage racism which exists in most other African countries is not an argument for it. But it is a fact that more than 85 per cent of black African people have no vote. Unelected governments wield power in Angola, Benin, Burkina Faso, Burundi, Cameroon, Cape Verde, Central African Republic, Chad, Comoros, Congo, Djibouti, Equatorial Guinea, Guinea-Bissau, Ivory Coast, Kenya, Lesotho, Liberia, Madagascar, Malawi, Mali, Mauretania, Mozambique, Niger, Nigeria, Rwanda, Sao Tome and Principe, Seychelles, Sierra Leone, Somalia, Namibia, Sudan, Swaziland, Tanzania, Togo, Uganda, Zaire and Zambia.

Mugabe has virtually declared Zimbabwe a one-party state and deals ruthlessly with the Matabele, hated enemies of his own tribe. Is this, then, to be the "solution" for South Africa? The black man who takes over the government of South Africa has a frightening responsibility to the world.

I do not know the solution to South Africa's problems. I do know that the simplistic — not to say, mischievous — proposition that to declare a one-man one-vote society with a sweep of the pen tomorrow would solve all, would, in fact, be disaster for all. I feel sadness that events in the country seem to be leading almost inevitably toward a bloody crisis. There seems to be little future for the white people and in the matter of carrying the can for history's law-makers they have little comeback. But they do not deserve to be lost and they do not deserve to lose what they have made their home. If they are lost so, then, is South Africa.

And as to playing rugby there with a New Zealand team I would defend the right to do so and I would defend the wisdom of it just as I believe the protest movement of 1981 would have done their declared cause much more good had the Springboks been able or allowed to move freely through this country and observe a way of life. There was much truth in the statement by the manager Johan Claassen at the end of the tour that to him the real tragedy of the tour was that young men who would carry significant influence in South Africa's future had not been able to see and feel the warmth of the New Zealand way of life.

I went back to South Africa in 1983 to play for Durban High School Old Boys till my return to New Zealand to try for the All Blacks against the Lions. And then in 1984 a Murray Mexted special, a totally commercial proposition through which I endeavoured to sell myself to companies as a promotions agent. I worked originally through Mr Endicott and Mr Evert Abendanon of the Johannesburg spoofers. They circulated business houses and sporting organisations peddling my wares.

At home people said I was dreaming. When I got to Johannesburg there were 100 letters waiting for me. I was selective and eventually linked up with a number of big companies who wanted me for public relations appearances at cocktail parties, motor-vehicle launches, client dinners, for speaking engagements, coaching seminars. The Sigma Motor Corporation sent me around schools including those for black or coloured children, coaching rugby, showing parents video coverage of the things I had done with their children during the day.

I guess you could say it was Mexted exploiting Mexted yet there was immense satisfaction in it. It was devised to give me another period in South Africa during which I could spend more time in sun and surf without being intensely involved with rugby. I was not in it to make myself a million. I charged myself out carefully so that my airfares and my living expenses were covered and I was assured of transport. One of my assignments was to attend a party in a private box at Ellis Park, drink champagne, talk with incredible animation with 25 of the company's top clients, discuss the match as it unfolded before us and generally have an all-round good time.

I sold loos down gold mines for a company which previously had not been able to get their foot in a door jammed with other feet. They wrote and offered my services and I became an instant expert in underground flushing. The guys at the mines were speechless. They saw very few people let alone a current All Black number eight. One mine captain said he could get me to sea level in the time it would take me to down the beer I had in my hand. I looked dubious. He jammed a hard hat on my head, took me into an ancient-looking cradle lift and pulled a handle. We dropped 6000 feet without our stomachs and into an eerie, science-fiction world. Another planet, another life.

The Coca-Cola company asked me to go to a rugby coaching camp at Umtentweni, a most beautiful resort at the mouth of the Umtentweni River. This was idyllic, a beautiful beach with a right-hand point break . . . and coaching South Africa's most promising schoolboy players. As I talked to them and showed them, I hoped that my approach, typifying rugby outside South Africa, would rub off on to them, that something would click so they understood rugby did not have to be all ball-protection and boot. If there is no enjoyment in playing the game outside some sort of glory-in-strength satisfaction then South Africa is going to suffer as their kids look elsewhere for their relaxation.

For a devout beach-bum that period at Umtentweni was paradise-found and through it, a year later, Umtentweni was going to exert an influence on my life I could not then have dreamed of. But that is another story.

During my 1984 visit I played my rugby for The Wanderers in Johannesburg, a magnificent sporting club which, in rugby, endeavoured far beyond other Transvaal clubs to play the running game. For Wanderers I played my last serious rugby in South Africa and with the job satisfaction I had as well as Umtentweni and the opportunities to chase the tubes at Jeffreys Bay way down in the Cape it was my best year in South Africa.

The year that wasn't

If 1984 was my best experience in South Africa what might South Africa '85 have brought? When I flew out in 1984 I knew the All Blacks would tour the following year and that I had a strong chance of being in the team. That was every All Black's dream — to play the Springboks in South Africa and beat them. From the time I became an All Black that was the vision, the ultimate challenge.

I was furious in 1980 when under severe political pressure the New Zealand Olympic Games team for Moscow disintegrated. This was to be **their** ultimate challenge. For years they had prepared themselves for it, fine-tuning their bodies and minds for the contest with the greatest athletes in the world. Russia went into Afghanistan. Governments told their athletes not to go to Moscow. Five years later Russia is still in Afghanistan and we are hosting the Russian soccer team in New Zealand. So we should. The crime was the original one, the politicians perpetrating exactly the interference for which they had criticised the black African countries which withdrew from Montreal.

Oddly enough there were politicians, too, who called for a withdrawal of Government pressure on Olympic sportsmen. Labour politicians like Richard Prebble and Ralph Maxwell . . . In a joint statement they said such things as, "It would be a tragedy for the New Zealand Olympic Games organisation to give in to the National government's blackmail and brute political force which have been used against individual athletes . . . the Government's pressure on sponsors, the dismissal threats to civil servants, and the cutting of wages are abuses of power . . ." The MPs sent a telegram to the Olympic and Commonwealth Games Association urging it "to resist National government blackmail and strong-arm tactics against individual New Zealand citizens' rights to travel wherever and whenever they wish. We consider the National government's actions in threatening wages and jobs of civil servants and bringing pressure to bear on sponsors is quite wrong, undemocratic and foreign to our way of life."

Bravo indeed. Applause from my corner. But feeling as strongly as they did then was there not a case for Messrs Prebble and Maxwell to be as vociferous and as indignant over the Labour government's pressure and strongarm tactics against the New Zealand Rugby Union and its players five years later?

One day one of the politicians responsible for the Moscow debacle must try to explain precisely what was achieved, what action outside sport New Zealand took to embarrass the Russians. Did we stop selling them wool? Stop importing their cars? Inject venom into their vodka potatoes?

Likewise, are New Zealanders not putting gold into their teeth any more or diamonds on their fingers? Is it not true that everyone can have what they like — everyone, that is, except sportsmen? That lady in the front rank of protest was wearing a South African diamond on her finger and the man beside her South African gold to plug up the unsightly gap in his teeth. But by playing rugby in South Africa I am condoning its political system. There's something selective in the state of New Zealand. One, two, three or a dozen people may come to New Zealand to assist the protest movement. The media faithfully record their stories as they should. But where does news begin and end? When is news not news any more because it has already been reported, printed and circulated? In one form or another newspapers reported the same stories time and again. But there was markedly less eagerness to record anything positive about the initiatives being taken by sporting organisations in South Africa to pre-empt changes in the apartheid laws. And if the country was evenly divided on the tour why feed fuel to one half of the readership and not the other?

When the Chief Justice, Sir Ronald Davison, brought down his decision that a High Court action aimed at stopping the tour should not proceed it seemed to laymen like myself that it was a decision taken fairly on the evidence. But when on appeal the case was turned back then, I suppose, anything was possible. And when Mr Justice Casey brought down his judgement which seemed often to drift into hypothesis that was proven to be so.

When the New Zealand Rugby Union council declared the tour to be on it did so, I believe, on a 13-5 vote. Media supposition that the council was evenly divided on the tour was hopelessly adrift. The Prime

Minister's adviser, Chris Laidlaw, was extremely active about this time. He rang all the NZRFU councillors on a number of occasions as he sought to ascertain how each would vote on the tour, and he asked councillors not to press for an early decision. It may have been that even then legal intervention was planned should the council vote to tour.

As I understand it, the council's meeting with the Prime Minister at the Beehive the day he departed for his tour of African states, resulted in deep anger among even the most moderate of the rugby administrators. They could not believe his demeanour which they found offensively patronising and there was a feeling that he was over-acting some stage role he had allocated himself. Some councillors were sure he had been told by Chris Laidlaw that they were evenly split on the tour and that eventually that would result in the tour being abandoned. As the Prime Minister left what the councillors found a totally unsatisfactory meeting he was still giving out with irrelevant one-liners.

The council ballot of 13-5 in favour of touring was taken first on an open vote though some councillors argued strongly in favour of a closed vote. In a subsequent closed vote I understand the same figures were recorded though not necessarily with the same individual division.

When the decision of the Chief Justice went to appeal it was strongly felt within the rugby administration that the appeal would fail. When it did not there was still confidence that the final decision would restore Sir Ronald Davison's judgement.

The injunction of Paddy Finnigan and Philip Recordon was based on the rugby union's constitution as it related to the good of the game. I have always had the feeling that the decision of the Auckland Rugby Union to come out in opposition to the tour because of the damage it would do to grassroots rugby, was a telling but ill-founded factor in the seeking of an injunction. In fact, I felt so strongly about it that when Wellington played Auckland I decided the right thing to do was say so. My after-match speech laid it pretty firmly on the Auckland Rugby Union that its duty was to the players of the game not to go public with pronouncements on evidence which was hypothetical. The chairman of the Auckland Rugby Union, Malcolm Dick, replied for the defence and honour was left unsatisfied. Much was made during the case and in the judgement of the disastrous consequences for New Zealand rugby of the 1981 Springbok tour. That would suggest a dramatic downturn in the numbers playing the game. But in school rugby there was no steep decline if decline at all. The net profits of the New Zealand Rugby Union were higher in 1982-83-84 than before 1981.

The cost to the New Zealand Rugby Union of the defence of their position has been something like $200,000. It could become more. Legal fees for this sort of protracted action are sky-high. I have no idea how Messrs Finnigan and Recordon settled up though it is strongly suggested very substantial public companies became involved and that solicitors gave their time freely.

The Saturday Mr Justice Casey was to give his judgement, July 13, I was playing for my club against Hutt Valley Marist on the Polo Ground in the suburb of Miramar. This time next week I would be under the sun on the hard grounds of the Free State. The game finished, handshakes all round, not too tired, nothing that a hot shower and a beer with the boys wouldn't cure. As I walked off our quite outstanding coach and good friend Alan Muir came toward me. He gave me a thumbs-down. It simply didn't register. We hadn't played too badly, I thought. I asked Alan what was wrong. "The tour," he said. "The tour's off."

I couldn't speak for a few seconds. It was as if I was in some time vaccuum. I realised I was staring at him. Then what came out was a strangled sort of demand that he stop talking bullshit. He repeated it, "Sorry Murray. The tour's off. The judge found against the rugby union." I needed something or someone to lash out at, then a physical draining as if I had played myself to a standstill and watched a test taken away by a dropped goal in injury time.

Under the showers there was none of the usual after-match banter. We went back to the club-rooms. Murray Pierce and I received presentations — the usual gesture by a club like ours to All Blacks going on tour. I felt strangely disorientated as I accepted mine. I spoke with lawyers in the club, to Nigel Hughes, the lawyer in the senior team. I became more and more despondent.

The following morning Brian Lochore, coach for the tour, rang sounding deeply depressed. No one may ever know how severely the cancellation of the tour hit him yet his immediate concern was for the players. He rang all 30 that day.

You start asking yourself questions. Why have I carried on? Why have I trained so bloody hard? Seven years an All Black and always the ultimate goal . . . now it has been snatched away. By whom? Assuming I am a law-abiding citizen should I not be entitled to travel where I want? How come at this very moment New Zealand is playing a squash test against South Africa in South Africa? All that abuse of myself and my family and any other Mexted who happened to be in the phone book . . . why should those cowards come out smelling of roses?

Everyone had been talking "rights". The "rights" of this group the "rights" of that, pondering without knowledge what effect the tour would have on the black people of South Africa, on law and order in New Zealand. No one seemed to be talking about the rights of the players, their families. In the welter of debate about the "rights" of every Tom, Dick and Harry the individuals most effected by the decision were forgotten. I presume our "rights" were equal to those of the two lawyers who brought the action, equal to those who saw us as morally corrupt because we wanted to play rugby in South Africa.

Morally bankrupt? Thirty athletes who had achieved the highest honour in their country's national sport. Thirty farmers, labourers, car salesmen, school teachers, policemen, doctors. We did our part for society daily and, I would think, more conscientiously than most of those who abused us. We got out of bed in the morning, showered, shaved, performed life's natural functions, ate Weetbix, meusli, bacon and eggs, went to work for eight hours — or 10 or 12 or more — went to rugby practice, went home to our families, talked of the day's events, laughed at life's little inconsistencies, made jokes about the latest political gaffe, got angry at the price of bread and milk, squabbled over a game of scrabble, stretched at the end of the late-night movie, pronounced ourselves weary, brushed our teeth, showered, went to bed, slept soundly or badly and woke to a new day.

That's what sort of people we were — and are. And isn't that what tour protesters were doing? And judges and lawyers? And most decent law-abiding New Zealanders — give or take the footy practice?

So in the essentials of being good citizens we were as good as the next bloke. Maybe even better than some. But did **we** really have our day in court? Were we setting out to destroy the game of rugby in New Zealand? Like hell we were. By beating South Africa in South Africa we would have done more for New Zealand rugby than by being told to stay at home.

When the New Zealand Rugby Union cancelled the tour the players met in Wellington and talked the whole mess through. We said we would all be available for an alternative tour but designated Argentina as the preferred country. But then the union found it was not possible to organise a replacement. So the players decided to go to South Africa as an invitation team. Everyone would go. No doubts. No reservations. Brian Lochore, as a servant of the union, could not be a part of the plan so we would travel under Andy Dalton.

Money was not the prize though there was strong suggestion we would all benefit very substantially. We were going as an invited team to play under the normal tours agreement. Assembly was in Auckland. Complications? Of course. But we'd sort those out. Hadn't the Prime Minister himself said we could go to South Africa as individuals, link up there and play as All Blacks or anything else?

I was in Wellington organising the Canterbury players. The rest of the North Islanders, other than Murray Pierce and Mike Clamp were in Auckland and so was Craig Green. The Canterbury boys travelled by private car to Picton and there, outrageously incognito, they boarded the ferry and arrived in Wellington about 4pm on Monday, July 22. Physiotherapist Peter Stokes picked them up at this end and they were to stay overnight in Wellington. Murray Pierce and I would go to representative training as normal.

I met the Canterbury contingent but by now South Africa was in emergency and some of the players in Auckland were having second thoughts. It was seen as unwise to go on with it. Tour off. The boys in Wellington had a few drinks and advised Grizz Wyllie they were available for their match against Wairarapa-Bush. So he whipped Victor Simpson into the team and placed Wayne Smith and Warwick Taylor in the reserves. Jock Hobbs notified his relieved wife he'd be staying home after all and everything seemed to be clear-cut.

Tuesday morning. Tour on. After telephone calls to and from South Africa the players having second thoughts decided to go. Complications: Vic playing for Canterbury, Wayne and Warwick in the reserves, Jock having reassured his wife he would be home.

We reorganised. Those involved with Wairarapa-Bush would come back to Wellington and I would drive them to Auckland early Wednesday morning and we would fly out for South Africa separately that night. So, on Tuesday, a private jet arrived at Paraparaumu Airport, 50-odd kilometres north of Wellington, its mission to collect three 007 passengers. The brilliant little jet arrived, we chucked bags over the fence, Albert Anderson, Mike Clamp and Murray Pierce went over after them, Pierce's wife waving goodbye, the pilot shaking hands with everyone, me shaking hands with everyone and saying, "See you in South Africa." It was the quickest farewell in history. And one of the most futile.

I drove back to Wellington, excited by the prospects. But it was deflation day all over again. That evening the players in Auckland, within a couple of hours of leaving for the airport, were advised that Ted Thomas QC, solicitor for Finnigan and Recordon, had telexed the rugby union solicitors stating that any breach of the court order would be met with action for contempt. Thomas wrote: "Our instructions are to act promptly against any subterfuge or connivance designed to circumvent the injunction." There was suggestion that Andy Dalton and Andy Haden could be construed as servants or agents of the rugby union — Dalton being on one of the union sub-committees and Haden its marketing consultant. The players met again, virtually as travel tickets were being delivered, and voted, not unanimously, to cry off. The withdrawal of the captain and the most senior player had taken the spice out of it. And going to South Africa with less than a powerful winning chance was not in anyone's script.

When the bitterness became less intense I sometimes wondered what might have happened if the rugby union had defied the judgement. Thirty All Blacks and the whole New Zealand Rugby Union council thrown into jail? That would, indeed, have made an ass of the law.

The Tuesday night the axe fell I went to club training, arriving late and, of course, with Pierce already being in Auckland. The players were stunned. They had assumed we were up and away. It was the most difficult training session of my life. Though I had peaked fitness for the tour there was neither the will nor the vitality to pick up the pace at training. A few of our planned moves were not going well. I lost patience and walked from the field. All the players, including my brother Alan, watched me go, understanding my problem and probably a bit embarrassed by it. I had walked about 20 metres when Bob McCarthy, our second five-eighths and a New Zealand Maori representative, came after me. He said, "Come on. This isn't you, Murray. Let's get on with it." Damn right. I went back, apologised and got on with it.

The next day I drove to Auckland anyway and Lorraine Downes and I announced our engagement. We had been engaged since April but I would have no part of placing her under the disgusting pressures of the lunatic fringe protesters while I was away in South Africa.

After the next Wellington representative training session we had a team meeting. Scotty Crichton stood up and made a pretty speech . . . "On behalf of the boys I'd like to congratulate you and Lorraine on your engagement. On behalf of myself I'd like to say that if ever you get into wife-swapping my phone number is on the team list."

Argentina — the new challenge

One of the great pub games used to be guessing the players who were selected for the All Blacks to tour South Africa in 1940 but who, because of the war, never made the tour. I have listened to old-timers at the club debating not only the players but the prospective result of the test series. At least our team was known. Would it have beaten the Springboks? I have a correspondent who wrote to me in May of 1985 predicting we would take the series: 20-17 at Cape Town, 16-16 at Pretoria, 28-19 at Durban. He never did give me a breakdown of the scoring and scorers.

Before looking at what might have been in South Africa, 1985, it is relevant to consider Argentina, 1985, the tour which was not a tour, then was a tour, then wasn't, then . . . It could not, could never, replace South Africa as a challenge to the All Blacks. Here, there was no tradition, no harsh physical build-up to the tests through provinces setting out to make the All Blacks feel every match was a test. I do believe that had Brian Lochore not made a powerful appeal to all the players selected for South Africa to go to Argentina there would have been more withdrawals. I was in doubt till B.J's appeal was published in the New Zealand Times and I was so moved by it that I followed it up with a supporting statement.

The esteem in which the players hold B.J. Lochore is rarely matched in the player-coach relationship. He is a calm, measured man of the land and, above all, his sincerity and his concern for the players and the game made him a rallying point for the team when the trouble over South Africa was at its height. He won respect from the players where there has not always been respect in the past — in his ability to coach rugby. That may sound far-fetched but it is one of the more bizarre aspects of New Zealand rugby that the All Black coach has so rarely been a coach, has so rarely coached tactics, built moves, taken individual skills and released them through team patterns.

Before B.J. there was Bryce Rope, before him Peter Burke and before him Eric Watson. Like Bryce, Peter Burke was a natural gentleman and he recognised that within his scope, coaching an All Black team with Mourie as captain and with experienced players forward and back was a co-ordinating job. And in this he was skilled. Peter would stand off training and observe, and when the time came he would draw team training together. He was hurt, I know, during the tour of France in 1981 when it was put to him that he was playing no part in the preparation of the team for the second test, that it had become a Mourie-coached team. But he did for the second test preparation what he had done at all times and it was a valuable contribution. While he was coach New Zealand played 11 tests and lost two.

If Argentina was no replacement for South Africa it was a marvellous surprise and the rugby in the tests was free-ranging and physically competitive. At the end of the tour we knew that the top 30 players in Argentina are a match for any in the world and on a major tour of New Zealand there would develop an intense test rivalry. It will take a little time for the New Zealand rugby public to accept that the Argentines mount a challenge to the All Blacks which is just as threatening as the Welsh or even the Australians. There will be a gradual acceptance that now Argentina is not Porta nor Porta Argentina. Now Argentina has backs in whom Porta himself has confidence and that is a far cry from my first experience of their rugby in 1979.

Rugby will prosper in Argentina. They are passionate about the game and they have that Latin feel for it. If politically we are denied South Africa, and that seems likely, Argentina will take the gap if not really filling it. International rugby can ill afford to lose contact with one of its traditional countries. We are in danger of over-kill on some tours and that is bad both for hosts and tourists. The virtual elimination of South Africa from the schedule creates an imbalance which will seriously disadvantage international rugby.

The players of Argentina are quick to learn. Where once their forward competitiveness was limited to the scrum and the "bajada" pushing technique there is now a broad range of sophisticated attack and defence techniques. They have had a more-or-less regular relationship with South Africa and this has helped harden attitudes and instil understanding that the South Africans are vulnerable to wide attack and hard-running threequarters. This is the new dimension in Argentine

Scott Crichton on the rampage against Rosario during the 1985 Argentinian tour. Supporting him are Murray Pierce and Gary Whetton.

rugby. Someone, probably Porta himself, has said Porta is not with us forever. Porta is many things but not ageless. When he goes Argentine rugby must not be allowed to go with him. The signs are clearly there now that there is thought and action beyond Porta and that he encourages it.

We went without Bill Osborne, John Ashworth and Andy Dalton of the players originally selected to tour South Africa. Osborne was severely affected by the decision not to tour. He had already moved out of his Hamilton home, he had made an effort probably beyond that of anyone else to get himself right for a tour which he, as a former tourist of South Africa, saw as his last chance to "take" the Springboks. Being the sort of player he is he was fizzing to get into the midfield confrontation with John Villet and Danie Gerber. Bill went through all kinds of agonies to impress his claims on the selectors, even as far as going into the New Zealand trial at Invercargill when he would have been better to sit it out. In shocking conditions, he aggravated a hamstring injury, got an almighty boot on the hand and had such a bad day there were some prepared to write him off. One critic told me, "Osborne's history." A bad judge. He would have been one of our great pluses in South Africa.

What Lochore was able to do immediately with his team was convince every one of them that he was there as a test prospect. When the team for the first test was announced in the hallway of the Buenos Aires Sheraton there was suspense. Almost every position had been opened up as a contest, including my own at the hands of Buck Shelford. It was tense but it was healthy and it was what Lochore had intended from the start. There was always the likelihood, considering the nature of the opposition and that it was the first test, that he would want to go into it with Haden, Shaw and myself so that with the touring captain, Jock Hobbs, there would be a team platform of understanding and experience. There was again this matter of height in the lineouts so that with Ure at 6ft 7 to contain I had the advantage over Buck Shelford.

Had Scott Crichton and Gary Knight not been injured it would have been a rare old battle for the test propping positions. Steve McDowell had thrust himself forward as a prime contender in any circumstances and Brian McGrattan, with that invaluable front jumping ability, was the one specialist loose-head in the party. Murray Pierce tipped out Gary Whetton on form and in the backs Victor Simpson was such a volatile, quick-thinking midfielder that he seemed tailor-made for this, a sort of Kiwi-Latin.

The selection of the Kirk-Fox combination behind the forwards was based, I'm sure, on Wayne Smith's sickness. Had Smith been fit, and considering Dave Loveridge's form the match before I could not envisage Lochore going beyond them as a pair. Yet Kirk and Fox played handsomely and Kirk's bustling ability to exert pressure and to take advantage of his own kicks were great assets. This may seem, then, to pre-suppose that I would support the retention of these two for the second test. In fact, I saw Lochore's decision to go for Loveridge-Smith as a brilliant piece of selection.

The first test was a beautiful expression of rugby, a great advertisement for the game in a country where it is developing rapidly and where, as the Pumas status internationally grows, more and more people are taking an interest in what has been a rich-man's sport. Rugby will never supplant soccer as Argentina's field sport but it will thrive.

Though we took a distinct advantage in the possession phases Argentina won enough ball for the backs to grow wings. There were centres like Diego Cuesta-Silva and Fabian Turnes who ran with that liquid elegance which characterises rugby in the Latin countries. Deceptive, though, this running because it was punctuated by sharp acceleration and by foot-skills and by alertness to the main chance — the gifts which distinguish the fine player from the adequate. Porta quite deliberately gave his threequarters latitude as he sensed the concentration we turned to him.

In the second test he knew we would move to plug the spaces and

Brian McGrattan, Gary Whetton, Scott Crichton and Andy Haden endeavour to prise news from the Spanish language newspapers in Buenos Aires.

that meant we would spread our defence. So he took much more of the game on himself, more kicking, playing for territory. He knew that he now had players of such ability outside that we could not sacrifice two loose forwards to him alone. Clearly we should have changed our tactics on Argentina ball. Jock Hobbs and I had to put pressure on him at the expense of wider cover. Our secondary pressure on him through Dave Loveridge was good. And this is one reason why I say the selection of Loveridge for that match was clearly thought through.

He reads Porta like a book and it was his quickness to understand Porta and to predict him which should have given us the winning of that test after the Porta-inspired comeback in the second spell. And if you think we should have had the test won through our half-time advantage you're right. Of course we should. In the meantime, though, we have a scrum near the Puma line with about ten minutes to go. Porta receives, he moves out of Hobbs' tackle but Loveridge has read his next characteristic feint and takes him to ground, ball and all. So it is our scrum at five metres and to the left of the posts. We can score. We should score.

I receive three different calls. The first is from Loveridge that I should have a go from the back of the scrum. Through the Mourie-Dalton eras of captaincy the five-metre scrum call is Dave's. So here I will have a go at the line and at best I'll score and at worst we will have another scrum. But suddenly the move is overcalled by a "lefto" in which I pick up the ball at the back, pull in their half-back and flanker and pass through the tackle to Dave who has drifted wide to the left. Dave pulls in their winger and our's scores. Simple. We've done it so often. Not a bad idea at all, I think. But the call is changed yet again for a release to the backs. And that is what we don't do. The impetus has gone with the changes of call plus a scrum collapse, there is a relaxation and Argentina strike for the tight-head hook and win it.

It was, in the vernacular, a balls-up. Too many calls, too many callers.

Earlier in the match when we were riding high we had a "lefto" call, but the ball was slow coming back and their half-back had shot off to shadow Dave. So I held the ball in, called for an extra push and our scrum lurched forward. I had only to control, scoop and drive over for the try. It shows there have to be exceptions to the call as events overtake intention.

When I came home I found widespread criticism of the decision to play Dave in the second test, that there had been a noticeable deterioration in the speed of his service, that it was crazy to change a winning combination and, above all, that he had a go on his own and failed to score when we had the big overlap out to the right. Because I was there, staring in close-up at what actually happened, I know that Dave should have emerged the national hero for that decision. It is a split-second decision and half-backs above all other players sniff instinctively the time to go. Dave did it. And he scored a try. He was not awarded a try but from my vantage point he certainly scored it. Such is the fine line between good and bad publicity or informed and uninformed public comment.

Between a number eight and a half-back there is a meeting of minds, a relationship unlike any other on the rugby field. Each develops an intuitive sense of the other's requirements or intent. When a number eight plays as often as I have with Loveridge there is an almost spiritual quality to that understanding. I consider it a privilege to have played

Jock Hobbs . . . leader of the All Blacks to Argentina.

with as fine a rugby player as Trapper. I should not express that sort of tribute alone. He deserves obeisance of some sort from all the bad lineout forwards he has made look good through his uncanny ability to cover shockingly-delivered ball and clear it. Making bad ball good ball is an art-form for a half-back and he has been the supreme artist.

There is artistry in Loveridge dictating terms down the short side, the games he plays with a defence as he plans the clear run for his wing. Loveridge's adventures with the French defence before he sent Stu Wilson away for a try in the Paris test of 1981 should be required viewing for every young half-back . . . first the scrum and Loveridge running hard and wide to the right, beating the flanker as if he were nailed to the turf, scooting clear of the close defence, coaxing Wilson's marker into some sort of hysteria, then, as the French seem to have him squeezed, a dummy — a mere gesture — and he slides through the bit of a gap he has won for himself, with a half-flourish of the hands he switches-off the man between himself and Wilson and flips the ball over to the winger for the complimentary sprint to the line.

Kirk showed on this tour that he has become a mature international player. The timing and velocity of his burst from scrum, ruck and maul is an outstanding feature of his game and he could still achieve the incredibly swift clearance of the ball of Loveridge at his best.

My criticism of the All Black performance in the second test is that we duffed it mentally. When we had scored four tries in the first spell and were leading 18-9 at half-time there was only one way to go. We had to open up, take the game so far out of reach that even Porta's magic boot would not pull us back. But we closed down. We originated nothing where we should have been originating everything. We had practised a variety of tap-penalty moves throughout the tour, saving them for the tests, but when the time came to use them we discarded adventure for ultra-conservatism. I regret to say we deserved what we got — a draw.

If, on reflection, there is some consolation for someone out of it, that draw was a win for Argentina. It will do the game immeasurable good there, make heroes out of rugby players so that small boys will be Porta and Cuesta-Silva and Turnes and the identical-twin wingers Juan and Pedro Lanza. Those identical twins! Juan and Pedro were so alike that it was strongly rumoured in Buenos Aires they played games with each other's girlfriends. Bedroom games.

The tour was surprising because Argentina was not at all what we expected. From his touring background in 1976 Andy Haden gave us a briefing and we expected a pretty rugged existence in a police state, curfews, street confrontations. What we found was freedom of movement, a wonderfully warm reception, the young people proclaiming their "democracy". We found fine food. The meat of Argentina was a show-stopper — the beef was all fillet-tender and rump-flavour, the steaks of such size that a rural trencherman like Albert Anderson had to declare himself defeated halfway through a meal. We were game for anything — stuffed intestines, suspected testicles, goatmeat taken from some surprising parts of the goat-anatomy. The one dish in an eight-course meat banquet which we suspected were the testicles of an unidentified beast were nibbled timorously rather than taken by the mouthful, chewed and swallowed, you will understand, but we tried.

There was luxury and there was squalor — such squalor and poverty

Rugby players don't go hungry in Argentina, one of the great beef-eating nations of the world. After training at Cordoba the boys rip into a meal prepared (above) barbecue style.

as you would not find in Soweto. Outside Buenos Aires there was still a strong militaristic line in the administration and we found, in our small way, that justice could be bought and sold. David Kirk and Robbie Deans were playing pool in a bar and the fun became a little rowdy. This rather upset the publican who in turn rather upset David and Robbie who, in such circumstances, were not prepared to kick for touch. The police arrived and they were taken to the local lock-up where many threats were issued . . . but, maybe, for a small consideration we could forgive and forget. But just this once, of course, for we are not truly corrupt, not in the sense of being, well . . . **corrupt.** You will see we have these hot little cells; notice the concrete floor; observe the bucket for all your toilet requirements. Desirable, is it not? No, you say? How much did you say? Well, in the circumstances . . .

And a pretty ruffled Kirk returned to the hotel 25 bucks lighter, but wiser, too, in that he now knew that the more moderate systems of Buenos Aires had yet to percolate through to outlying areas like Rosaria.

As opposed to the concrete cells of Rosaria there was the penthouse at the Buenos Aires Sheraton where Steve McDowell, Andy Haden and I were royally entertained by a rugby-loving Englishman who happened also to be administrative manager of Sheraton Hotels for the continent. We lay back and luxuriated, talked about rugby, quaffed with increasing recklessness his fine champagne and observed with studied insolence the hotel senior administrators playing the crawling sycophant to their boss. They seemed nonplussed to find us there, a group of New Zealand footy players acting as if they owned the show. But thereafter they treated us with embarrassing respect.

Brian Lochore introduced a totally new player-press relationship on that tour, new certainly in my experience if not in his. I think it was modelled on the common-trust basis of his own first tour with Wilson Whineray's team to Britain and France in 1963-64. On that tour, with a small media group — only four — there was a quite deliberate effort to make them part of the team. It was successful. As media groups on tour grew through the years so did the distance placed between them and the players. So much so that when I started touring the media were to be regarded with suspicion, not to say distrust. Obviously, there were individual exceptions, media people the players had found they could trust, but mostly the senior players passed on to the young players the attitude of "distance" if not animosity and a cycle was established. My own sensitivity to reporters had been established when I was a young player and I found that what should have been perfectly straightforward, harmless interviews were set down to put me in the

The All Blacks' new-look test front row in Argentina — Steve McDowell, Hika Reid and Brian McGrattan.

worst possible light. It was, as Eric Watson might put it, smartarse stuff and quite a lot of it goes on still through writers the players see to be fly-by-nighters, those who fly in for a story and fly out again damned quickly and may not be seen again for months.

The New Zealand media has been through strange spasms when it has been the in-thing to put down rugby. And the most convenient way of doing that was to put down the players as mindless cretins, which seems an odd way to go for a craft dedicated to objectivity and which judges itself to be high-minded in the pursuit of its creed.

We have big-noters in every field. We have All Blacks who big-note themselves and we have reporters. Players absorb criticism easily if they see it to be fairly placed and constructively explained. But the stories which are written unashamedly for effect and under the maxim that facts should never be allowed to destroy a good story make sportsmen puke. I feed news items to reporters I know can be trusted for fair presentation. One doesn't look for favourable treatment, just fair.

The All Blacks in Argentina set up a media committee and there was a conscious effort to make the group a part of the whole show. The signs were that it was appreciated and goodwill was reciprocated. Maybe it was the beginning of a new ball game between media and players. We will never be free, I know, of the snipers who stand off from rugby and play their own egotistical little word-games with it. Rugby has played a strong part in New Zealand's social development. It continues to do more for the children of the country than any other sport. I suppose that makes it some sort of target, but a psychiatrist would have to analyse why.

Since he was a young All Black, nudged aside by senior players who appointed themselves to the back seat of the bus, thereby proclaiming themselves a group apart, Haden vowed that when he became a senior there would be equality. He has set the example for many senior players now. What goods are presented to the team on tour are for **all** the team, what is good for the captain is good for the youngest players. This was another reason why I put the Argentina touring party above all others I have been away with — it was a team in every sense. In the merging of senior players and young it was just about the last word in everything Andy Haden had planned through the years. It was so from management right through. Dick Littlejohn was a players' manager, never setting up a NZRFU v The Players barrier such as we had experienced before. And B.J. Lochore must continue to be an influence in New Zealand rugby for every reason under the sun.

As I look back on Argentina '85, I think this was the team, this the coach, this the manager which, under Andy Dalton's leadership, would have gone to South Africa and won.

I look at players on the tour and I am aware that on an extended tour of South Africa, with that constant hard edge of competition, there were among them those who would have established themselves as the new All Black blue-chips of the late '80s and into the '90s. Steve McDowell stamped his authority on his opponents. If he can handle his success coolly and attach himself firmly to the responsibilities which go with success then he is a stayer. Steve is a good scrummager now but will improve, he's mobile and a very assertive runner bursting to the line, merges in aggressively on the drive.

Bruce Hemara was not selected to go to South Africa but when Andy Dalton withdrew he came to Argentina and confirmed his outstanding form of the All Black trial of 1984. He is committed and physically able to cope with the hard grind of top rugby but his greatest assets are his speed and anticipation and his ability to control his lineout throwing.

Brian McGrattan is one of those props who is sometimes underestimated by all except those who play with him and those who play against him. In a jumping area in which Wellington has thrown up some of the country's best players through the years he has established his claim

Wayne Shelford, challenger for the All Black No 8 position, scores at Cordoba.

as a long-term All Black.

Murray Pierce is the true number five jumper. As senior players move out of rugby and into their computerised offices I see Pierce retaining the five-spot while Gary Whetton becomes tomorrow's Haden jumping at three. To me Pierce is very much the Sam Strahan type of lineout man, capable of winning ball on any throw and reliability-plus from match to match.

Buck Shelford won his way into the team with a series of fine performances for North Harbour and, before that, for Auckland. I have said he was a contender for my place in the first test and so he was in every respect other than in the physical capacity to take on a man like the 6ft 7 Ure and win ball. Buck is a robust runner with ball in hand and in the final mid-week match of the tour when his confidence was running high he gave one of the most impressive individual performances of the tour as a running loosie. Buck is no spring chicken but I do believe he would better find his niche as a blindside flanker because as long as ball must be won toward the back of the lineout he will be at a disadvantage to tall young players coming through.

Grant Fox gets better as the occasion gets bigger. He was seen to be apprentice to Wayne Smith's tradesman but he had such a fine game in the first test when Smith was ill that it was agreed his apprentice days were in the past. I know he is eager to bring broader components to his game so that he is seen as a more versatile five-eighths; he likes to run with the ball but is more in the style of the one-break-a-game school.

One of the selections which created most discussion was that of Victor Simpson, the Canterbury centre. Playing for Canterbury Vic's trademarks were his aggressive defence, his ability to create sharp attack from broken play and his antagonistic frame of mind. He became a very good tourist and team man. No retreat with Vic, always prepared to give something a go.

I want to offer you the wingers as a bunch, as players who would have been outstanding successes in South Africa. All of them placed priority on keeping the ball alive and to players who might have covered 70 metres to get into a support position that is one of the greatest attributes in rugby. We have not always had wingers with that intent and though there have been brilliant try-scoring players there has been a tendency to die with the ball, to kill a movement stone dead because there has been too little concern for the other options. I suppose the most anonymous selection to the general public was that of Bryce Robins and the selectors were seen as having just another fling — as there had been in the past with some All Black touring wingers. But Cabbage Robins is not one of these. He is hard, fast, tough — an ideal player for South Africa. He revelled in touring as no other player in my time. He played each game as a test. I regret he came to the notice of the national selectors at such a comparatively late stage of his career. Mike Clamp, Craig Green (a great all-round competitor) and John Kirwan have years of international rugby before them but I would dearly have loved to see the quartet taking it to the South Africans in 1985.

I have said that the team, under the captaincy of Dalton, would have gone to South Africa and won. He is the only New Zealand captain other than Mourie in my experience who has the onfield capacity and who appears to carry the associated problems of touring captaincy with ease. I would rather play under Mourie or Dalton than captain a team myself. I like captaincy when there is no other better to do the job. I much prefer to be captain than be dissatisfied with one who does not measure up.

With Mourie you experienced the exhilaration of playing without fretting about the additional burdens of captaincy. Mourie gave players the freedom to take initiatives and this was not only a character-

Dave Loveridge and John Kirwan tangle with Rafael Madero during the second test in Buenos Aires.

builder for the individual but for the team. It is expressed in the All Black test statistics of Mourie's captaincy era. He was captain in 19 tests. New Zealand won 16 of those matches, the last ten in succession. It seemed to me there was always the possibility of having an exciting or entertaining match under his leadership and if there are those ingredients in a winning test the players' morale is sky-high . . . excitement, entertainment: add them to the efficiency without which test matches cannot be won and for the player in the middle you have total rugby. Whatever the activities of overseas touring which bring elation or even satisfaction nothing can match that comprehensive enjoyment on the field.

A captain's satisfaction from having devised and played a mental and physical part in a winning strategy is a dramatic extension of what the players under him feel.

Dalton is different from Mourie. There is an innate warmth about him. He does not need to place himself at a distance from a touring party, to maintain the aloofness which Mourie considered to be an element of captaincy. His ability to relate to people whether opposition, critics, fellow players, in what is an almost affectionate manner has gained him something more than respect. Something he projects creates rapport, whether with a group or with one of a dozen pressmen asking questions. I would like to think I could emulate Andy's composure in all the diverse circumstances of touring captaincy but I know I couldn't. As a player he is reliability personified, as dedicated to his team cause as any player I know. He has this desperate need to get to the ball on the ground. His effectiveness around the front of the lineout, the pressure he places on the ball and on the half-back are often underestimated. He "closes the gate" at that short end tighter than any other hooker in the world.

A touring captain has to have much more than leadership on the field and for all things I nominate Dalton as my number one all-round captain, a captain for all seasons and for all reasons.

It is one of life's enlightening experiences to play under the captaincy of Haden. The 1983 New Zealand trial in Wellington was Andy's piece de resistance. Not so much his captaincy during the game as in the preparation for the game. Our coach was one of the most engaging of rugby men — Neville Goodwin, RD6, Ashburton. Neville was full of high-rise suggestions, a bit like Bill Freeman when he wanted to bring some light relief to a hard training session. Bill would invent some crazy move . . . Scrum. Ian Stevens, instead of just passing to John Dougan flip the ball high in the air. Joe Karam, you come shearing up from full-back, take the ball and dive high over the scrum for the try. And it would be practised with high delight never to be used in a game.

I recall the Wairarapa-Bush prop Chris Kapene in gap-toothed wonderment as Neville explained the massive intricacies of a tap-penalty move. It was wonderland stuff, all imaginative deception and advanced mathematics but Andy determined Neville wouldn't be disappointed. So he called the move during the match and we actually had modest success with it. Andy, in mock euphoria over it, ran from the field, grabbed Neville and congratulated him on the success of the stratagem.

We had a big win in that match over Andy Dalton's team and it was here that Jock Hobbs made his plunge for Graham Mourie's open-flank position. His performance that day shot him into the All Blacks. I was so impressed with his commitment. He was seen by some to be another Mourie — "the new Mourie", they said — but to me he was more in the style of Leicester Rutledge and, to some extent, Kenny Stewart. There are not many Mouries in a decade of rugby. The flanker I see to be closest to the Mourie style is Dirk Williams, of Wellington, though he is not there yet.

Critics are given to tagging impressive newcomers with the names of champions. Gary Whetton was the new Haden. He arrived on the scene with a hiss and a roar, shunted along by press tributes which normally are reserved for players who have proven themselves champions among champions. But that is the modern way and I suppose it ignites public interest. I have said that Whetton's debut in that grotesque atmosphere at Eden Park in 1981, against a player with as awesome a reputation as Louis Moolman, was astonishing considering his inexperience. Now Gary is a five-year man. I sense he still has something in reserve, that there is more to emerge. But if it does not happen soon we may never see it. He has everything physically but he has still to take charge of a game as Haden, his mentor, can. I want to see all Whetton's abilities come together in one match and then consistently. He has been close to it on a number of occasions but the time is **now.** The whole circumstance of New Zealand forward play in the next year or two is a personal challenge to him as he becomes a senior player. As Haden, Knight, Shaw, Mexted ease out of top rugby New Zealand needs Gary Whetton with the added dimension of command.

The challenge for Whetton which would have plucked out that extra dimension disappeared into the air above the Supreme Court building in Wellington. South Africa 1985 was that challenge. Now he has to create his own and it should be every time he goes on to a rugby field.

Haden himself suffered from mindless comparisons with Colin Meads. He was never to be a Meads, not even from the beginning. Meads was never the classical, high-jumping ball-winner. He was the wrenching mauler who won lineouts by strength, almost by demand. Haden's talents were different from those of Meads in just about every respect and he became the player he is almost in spite of public demand that he should play like Meads. Andy often paces himself through a game — and in this he has similarity to Meads and to most big rawboned men who lock rugby scrums, jump in lineouts, heave into mauls and rucks and are expected in addition to get to the loose ball within a second or two of the loose forwards.

Sometimes he goes through the motions and often this is sufficient for a particular game. When the pressure is put on him — as it was by Mourie a couple of times — his response is always positive. But it is when he puts the pressure on himself that he lifts his rugby to those commanding performances as in the first test against Argentina and in Auckland's 1985 defeat of Wellington. The previous year Wellington had won the lineouts two to one against Auckland but here Haden took over the second spell and won everything. He has developed his own lineout style — something the Welshman Robert Norster has diligently copied. His concern at training that everything should be right, his emphasis on timing jump to throw, throw to jump. In ruck and maul he is happy to make his contribution as one of eight but never dictating as a Shaw dictates.

I can see Haden as an All Black manager, a brilliant one, though by then his company will be listed on the Australian stock exchange and he will be so busy taking over Brierly that the All Blacks may have to wait for another time.

"Great spirits," Haden will tell you, "have always encountered violent opposition from mediocre minds." Sometimes he confesses he's quoting Einstein. Other times he feels the truth of it so deeply you don't know where Einstein ends and Haden begins.

Beating the Boks, on paper

Having come through with the most fictitious prediction of all time (it was never going to be proved or disproved) I should say why I believe the 1985 All Blacks would have won the series in South Africa. It has to do with physical things like neutral referees — even if they were to come from the Home Unions — and our capacity to win enough possession with jumpers at 2,3,5 and 7, our ability to kick goals, the speed and strength of our wings . . .

But it has also to do with the spirit of the team as it emerged in Argentina. There was great team strength through this. When we failed to take control of the second test after achieving that big half-time advantage people back home were saying maybe it was a good thing we weren't playing a test series against South Africa. That fails to account for the build-up to the tests in South Africa, the programme of hard matches through which a touring team with the capacity of ours learns to sustain effort. From my experience in South Africa I have learned that to beat a strong side there you must win possession, preferably enough to dominate, but at least to be on equal terms. This team would have won, at the very least, equal possession.

All Black teams in South Africa in the past have suffered from inadequate goal-kicking — that necessity in modern rugby to kick goals from anywhere in the opposition half and beyond. In Fox, Crowley and Deans we had the greatest battery of goal-kickers any New Zealand team has had on tour. In 1976 we had part-time kickers trying to kick crucial test goals, we had novice round-the-corner kickers. In 1970 we had one of the most consistent of goal-kickers in Fergie McCormick but his range placed the All Blacks at a disadvantage compared with the booming kickers of the Springboks, Ian McCallum and Piet Visagie.

Robbie Deans (this page), Grant Fox and Kieran Crowley (opposite) . . . three marvellously accurate and proven goalkickers who would have ensured the 1985 All Blacks to South Africa didn't languish in the manner of their predecessors.

New Zealanders are great sportsmen but compulsive grumblers and the pubs, offices and factories ran hot with the condemnation of Kieran Crowley after his nightmare match in the second test against Argentina. Crowley had the sort of day every kicker has once, maybe twice, in an international career. Overall, the success rate through the careers of Fox, Crowley and Deans is phenomenally high and all can kick goals from distances which once made Don Clarke a freak among goal-kickers.

Our wings, as I have said, excited me and frustrated me. Excited me because I could envisage their success in South Africa and frustrated me because I knew they would not have the chance to show it.

This All Black side had a good weight of thinking footballers, many who could analyse conditions, trends in play, specify weaknesses, offer astute comment at team meetings. It had a coach acutely aware of the nature of touring rugby in South Africa, having captained an All Black team there, gone back to observe another All Black tour and back again to coach a World XV. It had a manager conscious of an old South African ploy to divide and rule. Touring teams in South Africa have often lost their managers, lost to the social whirl stirred up by hosts whose generosity is unmatched but behind which there are motives distinctly ulterior.

South African rugby does not encourage the thinking player. The coach is everything and, as most Springbok coaches are Afrikaners, there is a rigidity in planning which makes flexibility on the field a rarity. Witness the first test of 1981: adjustment, adaptability were just words once seen in a dictionary. The South African game is much more stationary than ours, a ball-protecting game as opposed to a mobile driving game. I have written of the deterioration in South Africa's traditional front row strength. The front-row confrontation is a phobia. It must be fought and won. There is no way the Springbok props I saw as recently as 1984 would control the Gary Knights, John Ashworths, Scotty Crichtons, Steve McDowells who were our original tour selections. The New Zealand front row in my time typifies the earthy durability and dedication of the All Black tight forward. I think of Knight as the archetypal New Zealand prop, going about his work conscientiously, sweating out every ounce in every game, master of his trade.

So, few South Africans would agree with my assessment of it. All other considerations apart, in the circumstances there had to be only one result for New Zealand: we had to win. I have heard Lochore say that after all the trauma of 1981 and the gathering up of opposition to 1985 it would be unthinkable to go and lose the series.

So a "World XV", an "International XV", tours South Africa. It will happen, of course. But where the towering pride of nation? A plastic badge beside a silver fern? It will be of passing satisfaction to South Africans. It will bring them notable players and it will bring the Springboks victories. But the heart will not be there and they will know it.

Danie Craven has said South Africa must hold out, must cling to its International Rugby Board affiliation so that the country's rugby will be protected for future admission to World Cup tournaments and

Gary Knight . . . no better prop in world rugby.

be realistically placed on the tours schedule. But the future of the amateur game in South Africa looks bleak. The players need more than provincial rugby and occasional invitation team tours to justify the sacrifices playing top rugby demands. Already there is a shift by leading players to English rugby league. That pressure will grow as league scouts recognise that here is a reservoir of unfulfilled union players.

Dr Craven has looked toward the South African Rugby Board's centenary in 1989: "Perhaps we will have our own world cup festival then.

But, number one, it must be an amateur gathering and, number two, it must be non-political in every sense of the word. I cannot bear politicians and I cannot bear people who will not stand up to them. When South Africa was in the doldrums we (the South African Rugby Board) were expected to fight our government. I was insulted, I was ordered out of offices . . . One government minister said to me, 'Craven, I despise you for the despicable man you are.' I replied, 'I'll take it whence it cometh.' I had to bear all that. It wasn't easy. We opened the way, far ahead of political thinking of those days. But having integrated our sport, having battled the politicians and defied laws before change, we are now blocked by the politicians of other countries. It is a bitter irony."

The tragedy of South Africa may well be spelled out in that message from Danie Craven — that where sport went politicians have feared to tread.

Politics, politicians, sport and tragedies were far from my mind one evening in Johannesburg in 1984 when I set out with purpose to meet a young New Zealander who had been warmly praised in a letter from my father . . .

Lorraine's story

I didn't actually say, "So what." But when this overpowering man put out his hand and said, "Hello. I'm Murray Mexted," and stared at me that's about how I felt. Murray Mexted? Murray who? I had just been introduced to someone named Don as if I should have known who he was. Don, they said, Don Clarke. You know. The All Black. Well, I didn't know. All Blacks were big rough people who played a game with a funny-shaped ball, got dirty, went into huddles they called scrums and had their after-match booze-ups. I didn't know a Clarke from a Smith, Brown or Jones. And I hoped this guy Mexted wasn't going to make a nuisance of himself. When someone said a few hours later "So you met the All Black?" I assumed they were still talking about Don Clarke. How was I to know there was an All Black named Mexted?

That was in Johannesburg, 1984. I was still on the Miss Universe roundabout and protected from the advances of designing males by my wonderful Mexican chaperone, Ruth Romero, who had an eye like an eagle and a mind like crystal in the detection of men who might become heavy. One of the things Ruth and I had in common was that we knew nothing, but **nothing,** about rugby and rugby players and cared less. Now in Ruth this was understandable. To her rugby was far removed from any aspect of life. But in me, Lorraine Downes, daughter of a rugby fanatic, and coming from Pakuranga, Auckland, New

Zealand, it might be considered some sort of heresy.

Poor Dad. The father of four daughters who didn't give a jot for the game he adored . . . "Who's going to get up early in the morning and watch the test with me?" Not me. Not me. Not me. Not me. I remember getting up in the small hours for a glass of water and seeing him, sitting over a cup of tea and a sandwich and staring at a screen on which there were bundles of men throwing a ball around. That seemed pretty foolish to me. For all the attention he gave to us and our interests that may seem a little selfish. But it's the way kids are and he didn't really mind, just shrugged it off with resignation and found other compensations in having four girls.

We were a very close family, did everything together — except watch rugby. Every man wants a son he can take to the rugby. Dad had to put up with going to netball and ballet recitals. Sometimes he would start to make conversation over the dinner table about Saturday's match, stop, look up, see four blank faces and change the subject. My mother and father, Gladys and Lloyd, were married young. Now their eldest daughter, Susan, is 30 and their youngest, Caroline, is 15, Jennifer is 26 and I am 21 and, other than the sisterly tiffs that happen in the teens, I can never recall anything but warmth and happiness in our home. We did not divorce ourselves from all my father's interests. He was very musical and during the '60s was New Zealand's champion cornetist. He never could quite understand how someone like me, loving music, feeling rhythm, dancing, could be so outrageously tone-deaf when it came to singing. Murray is the only person I know who can sing so consistently off-pitch as I. Together, they tell me, we sound so bad we are almost worth listening to.

Yet music has been a large part of my life. Once I planned a career in dancing. First it was ballet. I loved ballet. But I went into it so late that I was dancing with girls who were about half my size. I became quite self-conscious about this and it became clear, anyway, that ballet could never be my career. I had started years too late. But modern jazz dancing . . . **there** was another thing. Eight of us with the Julie Cotter Dancers danced at fashion shows and Telethon, and it became an enveloping influence in my life. It brought discipline to my everyday existence . . . exercises, learning new dances, practising, practising. It taught me that if you don't keep up to scratch you are replaced, and that applies to life.

My mother stitched and sewed like one of those fairy-tale seamstresses. She made all my elaborate costumes. When we did Star Wars with all that futuristic, spacey look she worked through the night. She turned

In raptures after being named Miss New Zealand at Christchurch in April, 1983. Marise Wipani, of Auckland, right, was runner-up and Marya Gratkowski, of Wellington, third.

this sort of devotion to all of us, no matter our interests. I always had a desire to teach and for two years taught modern dance classes. I found that I had swift sympatico with the girls, that there was such mutual understanding that teaching brought satisfaction as I had not known it before. I became involved in choreography, costume design and the more saturated in the work I became the more certain I was that there was a career there for me. I auditioned for television programmes and once got into a Christmas Special but it was University Entrance year and dancing had to come a long second to study.

One burning ambition I never fulfilled — to become a go-go dancer. As a child I always watched the television programme Happen Inn and my mother absorbed with serene equanimity my shrill resolve to become a go-go dancer. So, dancing filled much of my adolescent life but when it became clear the opportunities were too spasmodic to make a career of it I planned to become a school-teacher. When I had UE accredited I was elated. When they said I was too young to go to Training College I was devastated — you know, in the way teenagers become prostrate with disappointment or grief at personal crises in their lives.

Those primary and secondary school days were not **all** dancing. Though my ignorance of rugby seems to imply, in the New Zealand environment, a total lack of interest in sport I was crazy about athletics and netball. As a member of the Hillsboro Athletic Club I won the sprinting trophies through my young years — including one when I broke Kim Robertson's 60-metre record. Later I represented Howick as a netball goal-shoot. All of us loved sport.

In school Susan and I were the most serious scholars. I had to work hard. I was not the natural academic like many of my friends and I had to study to pass. Socially, I was a performer. All my teachers noted that in class I was a shy girl who did not contribute greatly to class discussions. But when I went on stage something I could not describe happened to me. There was confidence, I became expressively extroverted, there was in me a passion to perform. On stage I felt the sort of inner peace which is outwardly expressed by natural warmth. This was to be a telling quality for me one fabulous night in St Louis not too long afterward.

The sea was my other love. From the time I was a baby the sea was like a home. Every year at Christmas vacation the family took a caravan to Mount Maunganui and there we lived in the sea. I have no memory of nervousness or fear in the water, just of long, luxurious days — and **these** bathing suits did get wet. As we grew up it was with beachboy

Miss Universe contestants looking happy — but really being apprehensive — at a luncheon before the big night in St Louis in 1983.

At a Government reception back in Wellington after being crowned Miss Universe. Sir Robert Muldoon and Rob Talboys represent the Government, and the Downes family group comprises Mum, Dad, Caroline, Jenny and Susan.

boyfriends and I swear not one of them ever wanted to talk to me about rugby. The one thing above all else which made Murray and me click was our discovery of a mutual love of the sea and the sand. The beach to me is a spiritual place, the one place to be alone with my thoughts and in tune with them.

My secondary school in Pakuranga was co-educational. But I cannot even remember a first XV name. I can recall playing touch-rugby with the boys and I can remember thinking even that was miles too rough for me. But as for mad crushes on captains of first XVs, forget it. Not interested. None of us went out with rugby players. They were not part of our world. I'm sure Dad would have loved a yarn with a first XV number eight but we couldn't even deliver that for him.

One day in the street when I was in that school-leaving vacuum a man came to Dad and me and introduced himself as Max Thompson, a photographer. Modelling, he said. Your daughter has a good look for modelling. I'd like to take some photographs. About the same time Susan Rogers-Allan, a modelling agent, said much the same thing but added the all-important piece — "I think I can get you into full-time modelling." Now things were falling into place. Modelling for a year, then to Training College, maybe even university. So I modelled. For a year it was very successful, lots of television commercials and magazine ads. It seemed people wanted to see me drinking Coke and Lemon and Paeroa, wearing Pick-a-Berry. I just had the right look for the time, I guess.

I would not have thought of entering for the Miss Universe New Zealand contest. I didn't think of myself in that way at all. But I was planning to go to Sydney to model and the $500 for becoming a finalist was tempting. It was $500 toward establishing a career. So in I went. I have always rather lacked faith in myself and sometimes I found myself wondering what on earth I was doing among these lovely girls. But there I was in the finals. They announced the third place-getter and it wasn't me. Then second and I thought, well, that's it, back to Auckland for you, girl. Then I had won, and the enormity of it hit me. Not $500. Much, much more. Not Sydney via Auckland to scratch for a career. St Louis via Auckland and such wonders I could not dream of. I was 18. I had never been overseas. I realised how much of a close-family girl I was. I had always promised myself travel, envisaged myself as the confident girl out there exploring the big, wide world. Now the opportunity had come in such a rush that all the excitement could not quite disguise how good life in Auckland with my family was.

St Louis . . . on the Mississippi in there near the mouth of the Missouri. Established in 1764 by the French. Furs, livestock, grain. Population 620,000 plus the Miss Universe contestants. And plus their entourages. Yes, their entourages. I was a lone New Zealander — and I mean **lone.** So many of the other girls had their hairdressers, their makeup artists, their photographers, their back-up people. I thought, this has got to be some mistake. No mistake. And I knew then that when a New Zealander achieves she **really** achieves, because she does it all by herself. No other New Zealand girl had won Miss Universe. I knew I couldn't. These beautiful girls . . . all these professional girls, groomed and polished, their hair dressed and glossed by their specialist individual dresser, Miss USA, Miss Japan, Miss Brazil, Miss Sweden, Miss, Miss, Miss . . . front page pictures, radio interviews, television interviews, life stories, public polls. Me? No front pages, no interviews, no high marks from the public. Hidden away. Just a starter. Except that my dancing experience got me in the front-line of the show. No big deal? Well, it was **something.**

My room-mate was Leeanne Hoskin, Miss South Africa. When I arrived someone from the Miss Universe New Zealand organisation asked if I wanted to be shifted from Miss South Africa's room. I told him not to be so silly. I liked the lady and we became good friends. She was suffering from political pressure, too. And we both suffered from home sickness. We had boyfriends back home, we missed our families. There we were in that hot little room talking of our countries and people, talking of the contest, convincing ourselves we couldn't win, taking comfort from the minute possibility we might squeeze into the final 12.

The physical and emotional strain of the preparation was exhausting. Girls lay on the stage sleeping after rehearsals. It was a 6 am start every day, breakfast, rehearsals all day, back to our rooms at 5 pm, out at 6 pm to cocktail parties, receptions, meeting the media. We had chaperones, one to every two girls. They accompanied us everywhere. Everywhere? Yes, there, too.

Three nights before the final my mother and father arrived. If they hadn't I might never have been Miss Universe. That last week I was tired, emotionally wrung out, homesick and depressed. When they arrived it was like new life for me. I was lucky. I was shining again — I mean shining inside, and that makes the outside relaxed and happy. Winning was the last thing on my mind. Being there with my parents watching was everything. I remember standing on the stage of the Keil Auditorium. Out there, were 16,000 people. Around the world there were millions watching. And I was filled with the peace I had when performing as a young girl with my family in the audience. It was as if I was watching the show from the outside . . . "I'm not here. I've watched these shows on television since I was a baby. I'm not here . . ."

The greatest thing to me was that I was in the position of being able to say I was representing New Zealand. I could never represent New Zealand as an athlete or a scholar or, least of all, as a singer. But here I was representing New Zealand among girls from all over the world. When it came to the selection of the final twelve Miss New Zealand was first called. Then the final five — and a most peculiar, an almost psychic thing happened to me.

The Keil Auditorium is a vast tiered theatre. I stood there almost numbed by the event of being named in the final five. Somewhere among the 16,000 people were my mother and father. I had no idea where they were sitting. I looked up and directly into their eyes. In that communication I was sharing everything with them. It gave me, somehow, an extra oomph. I was so lucky — lucky because through that whole show it was never a contest to me. It was a performance and I was back there at school again doing my number on stage. The only nerve-wracking part of it was when I was called on to speak. I had butterflies, a thousand butterflies, but I knew that unless I relaxed and behaved and spoke naturally it would count heavily against me. Too many girls have failed by the nature of their speech and by the temptation to be "someone else" under interview.

Five became two and I stood there with Miss USA, 5ft 10, 36-24-36, supremely confident, needing to win and knowing she would. The crowd was behind her. She had been front-page day after day. She had the presence of a winner. I assumed she was. It didn't worry me; I was thrilled to be runner-up. Then the tension build-up ". . . and the winner . . . Miss Universe . . . 1983 . . . is . . . Miss . . . NOO ZEALAND!" There's a pause, like the silence in an auditorium in the second or two after a magnificent orchestral or vocal performance and then a wave of sound becoming a flood, then people, the tears springing, a sudden ridiculous concern they might smudge my makeup, as suddenly knowing it doesn't matter, turning, looking up to where mum and dad are, then a rush of thoughts . . . my life, what's happened to my life? . . . a year away from my family and friends . . . I'm Miss Universe . . . what are my friends going to think? . . . and what about poor Miss USA . . . the bedlam, the music, flowers, a crown on my head, a million kisses, what are they doing in Pakuranga . . .

So I became the property for one year of the Universal Corporation. I was to share a flat for a time with Miss USA and it became

Lorraine and these children got on famously — her warmth made her popular in southern Africa.

·rst, win the chaperone. Here, she is won. Ruth Romero, Lorraine's Mexican pro- ctor, left, the night of the Latin-American exhibition, Johannesburg, 1984.

The Victoria Falls proposal becomes public to New Zealand, six months after the event.

During the round-the-world courting — Tokyo, 1985.

Miss Universe, 1983 . . . after being crowned at the pageant in St Louis.

The big day, February 15, 1986 — Mr and Mrs Mexted.

clear that was not going to be so easy. Stricken with disappointment, having been told by her friends, her supporters, her family, she was a winner, her career depending on it, she refused to communicate. No talk; rejection when I tried to smooth the way. She seemed somehow scornful and it hurt. It took six months for our relationship to warm.

For a year my life was not my own. Nor were the prizes the Miss Universe title carried. They do not come unearned. I worked to exhaustion point for a year and it was not till the last six months that I found absolute confidence in myself as Miss Universe and as a woman. I learned in that six months that if you believe in yourself, have faith in yourself, nothing will stand in your way. I learned that insecurity engenders fear and that is oppressive to success.

Companies paid the corporation $2000 a day to have me do their promotions in their countries. In South America Miss Universe is queen of the world. They flock to the airport in their thousands to greet her, the bands play, the streets are strewn with flowers. Miss Universe time is carnival time. The press conference — now there's an intriguing vehicle for all sorts of political pressure questions to a lady who is there for just about every reason except the political one. I parried them by telling the truth. I was there representing the girls of all the countries who had participated in the Miss Universe contest. I was, I told them, an ambassador of peace, not of any political ideology.

Every day, work appearances, cocktail parties, hospital visits, orphanage visits, autograph sessions — one day I autographed 5000 photographs. Miss Universe never got tired. Miss Universe never failed to smile. Miss Universe never didn't talk to people. Miss Universe never had a bad day. Occasionally in her room Miss Universe broke down because she was physically and mentally exhausted. And she cried through the telephone to her parents in little Pakuranga, a million miles away. Mum became terribly worried at those times. Dad said, "She'll be OK in the morning." And I was.

After six months I had a break at home. Christmas, to Mt Maunganui for the day. But my life had changed. Everyone wanted pictures and autographs. My privacy had been overtaken by public demand. There was a small party for my friends. When I walked in everyone stopped talking, turned and stared at me. My friends . . . I thought, "I'm never going to be just Lorraine Downes again. I'm going to be Lorraine Downes, Miss Universe, even to my friends." I thought then that maybe I had lost my fight to stay myself, not to change at any cost. I had determined that when all the Miss Universe campaigning was over there would not be a sort of plastic Miss Universe who looked like Lorraine Downes.

It was on my second visit to South Africa as Miss Universe that I met this guy Mexted. I was there for the Miss South Africa pageant. There was a cocktail party at Ellis Park. The usual thing . . . I circulated, had pictures taken, met and smiled at countless people. Then the voice said, "Excuse me. Hello, I'm Murray Mexted." He was big. None of my boyfriends had been big. I had never been attracted to overwhelmingly big people. Then he thrust out his hand and started firing questions at me. "Who does this man think he is?" I thought. Then I thought, "I've got to move away. I want out." So I did. With no regrets.

Later, in the course of circulation, I met him again. He told me his father had written to him after the Miss Universe contest expressing pride that a natural New Zealand girl had won it. So he decided to front up and see for himself. He said he could see that in my position I was meeting a lot of people, going through the formalities and the trivial chit-chat, shaking hands and moving on. He said, "I felt I had to be a little forceful. Otherwise, you'd have moved on and forgotten me." I didn't say that had been my intention but he was less reluctant. He said that when we were talking he thought, "Well, she's nothing special." Big deal. When we spoke again he was different. No aggression, just another New Zealander far from home talking of the things he loved. We found we had a common affection for beach, surf, Mt Maunganui.

There were good vibes. When he said he would like to take me to dinner back home and walk the beach, I agreed it was a date. Next day there was a bouquet. I knew I was attracted to him but rather than any sort of elation that knowledge brought a feeling of pressure, complictions when I didn't need them. I didn't want that sort of involvement. So I didn't ring him, quite deliberately decided on silence. He rang, though, and I lied. I told him he had caught me just as I was going to ring him. Shameful. He said that was good because he had been about to tell me he thought I was bad mannered. The direct approach, honesty at all costs.

That night I had to attend an official dinner and planned to go afterward to a night club. I asked him whether he would care to come. Rugby practice, he said. Rugby practice! Second string to a sweaty scrum. Wait till Miss USA heard about this. But he would come along afterward. At dinner they told me the night club had closed down and we would go somewhere else. I couldn't get the message to him but he had the interest, at least, to do his own detective work and he found me and it eventuated that when I had been calling him he had been

We never really enjoyed the wedding . . . best man Peter Brookes, Downes sisters Jenny and Caroline.

within shouting distance in the same club.

They may talk for years about the floor show at the club that night, the night Murray Mexted, All Black, who had never danced Latin American in his life and might never again, performed like Fernando Lamas on one of his better nights. It was all cunningly contrived. Murray recognised his first victory had to be over Ruth Romero, my Mexican chaperone. Ruth, small, vivacious, skin like silk, temperamental, was, then, the target. When the music started he turned away from me and asked her to dance. Not being in on the scheme I regarded this with something less than warm understanding. It delighted Ruth, though, and no more than when the music started. It was Latin American. Murray looked slightly startled then decided that what he had seen in the movies he could copy on the dance floor. It was the hit of the night. He was down on his knees, clapping, swivelling. He was stamping, clicking his fingers over his head, darting passionate looks over his shoulder. He didn't miss a trick. And Ruth was won. A coup. But it went on and on till a gallant gentleman in the party took me on his arm, walked on to the floor, excused Murray, took over Ruth and left us together.

What followed was weeks of international telephone calls and many, many letters, months of meeting in many parts of the world, sometimes just fleeting, sometimes a few days. Our first meeting after South Africa was in New York. Murray travelled home via London. Part of his baggage was a surfboard. What else? He was coming on to New York by El Al, an airline so sensitive about security that he had to check in two hours ahead of flight time. They did not find Murray especially believable . . . "You are travelling to New York from London with a surfboard? Why? You have been to South Africa? Why? You are actually going to New Zealand? You came from South Africa to London to go to New York to go to New Zealand? Why were you in South Africa? To play rugby? What is rugby? You are a rugby player going to New York? Why? You are meeting a girl? You are taking a surfboard to this girl? No? We will X-ray your surfboard Mr Mexted . . ." And they did. They found him so unbelievable finally, that they knew it all had to be true. But had he told them his date in New York was with Miss Universe he might still be under restraint somewhere.

Our friendship was helped along by my mother and father. Murray quickly detected he had allies there. When I told dad I had been seeing something of an All Black named Mexted there was a distinct glow in his eyes. "Murray Mexted?" "Yes. Is he any good?" "Just the best there is." I had the feeling that from that time my father became a master

Room-mates from Miss Universe, 1983 — Leeanne Hoskin (Miss South Africa) and Lorraine are the beauties to my beast after the wedding.

match-maker and my mother his apprentice. Once, without any organisation, Murray and I arrived back in New Zealand on the same day — he from rugby in Fiji, I from two months of modelling in Australia. He was to leave for France the following night to sell scrum machines. Scrum machines . . . that didn't seem to make an awful lot of sense to me. What did they do? Turn a handle and out popped eight big hairy men numbered 1 to 8?

In the brief time we had before Murray went to France we had dinner together in a little restaurant in Auckland — our first public meeting in New Zealand. We were conscious of the whispers and nudges but more conscious of the bond which had grown between us. As soon as Murray returned, we decided, we would go to his little seaside haunt on Pukehina Beach, in the southern Bay of Plenty. We needed time together.

And that is what happened. There had been speculation in the papers but it seemed to be written almost as a matter of record so the paper concerned would not be seen to be second with any news. We wanted our privacy as it became clearer to each of us that there was a future together. While we were at Pukehina we decided to go to the Mt Maunganui Beachgirl contest, just a short trip and we would slip in the back hiding behind sunglasses. We did that. We were barely in there, confident we were incognito, when some sharp-eyed master of ceremonies actually announced us. And the next day the local paper ran a picture with the caption, "Who is this in the crowd, trying to hide behind the sunglasses?" No escape, it seemed. We went sailing around Golden Bay near Nelson for a fortnight and it was then that we decided to have our time together overseas.

In February, 1985, I had work to do in Tokyo. Murray called there for a couple of days and then flew off to London and on to South Africa. I joined him there and for two months we had our time together in South Africa, in Zimbabwe and Zambia. There were two gorgeous weeks at Umtentweni where Murray coached school first XVs. We were on the sand by 8 am and then every couple of hours between coaching classes and again in the evenings basking in 30 degree heat.

We flew to Zimbabwe at the same time Mr Lange and his retinue were travelling through Africa. It was just after he had been so critical of a small group of journalists who decided to leave the party and go through to South Africa for an interview with the foreign minister, Mr Pic Botha. We were booking in at Johannesburg Airport to fly to Harare when a man tapped Murray on the shoulder and said, "Murray Mexted? I'm from the Auckland Star . . ." and there was another from Television New Zealand. Murray muttered, "Put your sunglasses on, be inconspicuous." There were visions of the All Black-Miss Universe story splattered all over the front page of the Auckland Star and topping the television news. I pulled my head in, shrank to half my size, turned away, intent on filling in my departure card though now I couldn't absorb a word of it.

If they looked at me at all it was only with the appraisal that Murray Mexted had a girl with him. And that, on past history, was not news, was it? The Star man said, "We've just been down to see Doc Craven. We've been travelling through Africa with the Prime Minister and now

Players close to my heart with their wives on my wedding day . . . Andy and Trecha, Hewie and Pauline, Trapper and Jan, Bernie, Cowboy and Mandy.

he says as far as he's concerned we can swim home." He was quite unfazed by it all. He showed Murray the front page of the Johannesburg Star on which Mr Lange's statement was printed and he asked him to say a few words for publication. Murray was pleasant but refused, saying it was a private visit and he had no comment to make on anything.

We hustled off to our plane. But there was little respite there. The Kiwi newshounds were on the same flight. I slumped down with my face averted wondering why someone had not been inspired to make fashion sunglasses full facial. It was a flight I would rather forget though I had the feeling Murray was starting to enjoy the situation. At Harare we stood around waiting for our baggage, Murray looking one way, I in his shadow looking the other. As we went through Customs the officer said, "So, you have come here to see your Prime Minister?" Murray said, "No. We have come here to see the Victoria Falls." Then we were out and safe.

Zimbabwe was so romantic for us; the overwhelming beauty of the country snatched my breath. We drove from Harare to the Mozambique border in the eastern highlands, stayed on the verge of the Rhodes National Park. We went to the vast Wankie National Park, 13,000 square kilometres of north-western Zimbabwe, a place of tranquility and such wonderment among the animals, such closeness that there was a feeling, almost as strong as a desire, to reach out and touch the beauty of them. In their habitat there is a beauty in all animals — even the warthog — and here the breadth of species was flamboyant.

But it was somewhere else much less tranquil, within the sound and fury of the Victoria Falls, the wildest convulsion of water in the world, no fences, no ice-cream vendors, no "this way, ladies and gentlemen" — this was the place where Murray proposed. We had heard on the radio that the All Black tour to "the white dictatorship of South Africa" was on. We drank some champagne to that and later, the proposal. And the acceptance.

Murray was deeply concerned when we arrived home that the engagement should be kept secret because of his involvement with the tour. He feared the controversy could affect my work and my life. Quite outside that aspect of it there was scepticism among my friends about the durability of a relationship in which one party was in Auckland and the other in Wellington. Durability was sealed in our engagement and I couldn't tell them about it. So for weeks and weeks we kept up the pretence. Then the day after the tour was cancelled Murray came to Auckland and our engagement was public.

And what of rugby and me? I am learning about rugby and I am learning about misconceptions about the game and the men who play it. The first time I saw Murray play was just a little game in Umtentweni. When he ran on to the field with the ball in his hand there was instant excitement. The referee was a bit of a nuisance, I thought, blowing his whistle all the time, stopping them when they were running and telling them it was time for a scrum. A few guys on the sideline were saying terrible things about Murray and for the first time I was conscious that in a way Murray and I were in the same business. The lifespan of the model and the lifespan of the rugby player are short and both are always conscious they can be replaced. Sitting in the grandstand during a test I hear someone behind me saying something like, "Mexted, you mug." When my mother is in the audience at a modelling show she hears a lady behind her criticising my makeup, my walk, my stance. Murray and I realise how fortunate we have been to have success in our lives. We do not take it for granted. We work at it.

I love New Zealand and New Zealanders but they **do** proclaim you and claim you and put you up there on a pedestal, then suddenly knock you down. Murray has felt it and so have I. There's something terribly perverse and small-minded in the attitude to continuing success. Small errors are seen as gigantic blunders, personal mannerisms are a matter for ridicule. The Americans love their own, a star is always a star to them, the top achievement lives on. I am no analyst but I have heard of the great political clobbering machine and I wonder whether it is not more a national trait than a political phenomenon in New Zealand. I do know that those who clobber are often those who have achieved nothing.

I was terribly nervous about my first meeting with the wives and girlfriends of All Blacks. I was shown to my room which I was to share with Gary Whetton's girlfriend Jane. Most of the others had already arrived and were together in another room. I sat in my room for half an hour. I wanted so badly to be accepted by them but I felt I was the outsider. Well, it had to be done. I walked into the room, said, "Hello. I'm Lorraine" and Pip Dalton immediately broke the ice. From then on it was a fabulous weekend. We were a team ourselves. On the way to the game, the second test against England, our bus was deadly quiet. Every lady was feeling for her man.

When they ran on to the field the hair on my arms bristled and I shivered. I suppose that meant I was hooked. There I was, Lorraine ("What can you see in it, Dad?") Downes going crazy about a game of rugby. I suppose I have been lucky to come into the game with the new breed of players and the more relaxed attitude to the ladies from the administrators. Pip Dalton and Trecha Haden started in the days when ladies were seen as some sort of nuisance-appendage to the game. I have become very conscious, specially from visits to the Wellington Rugby Club rooms, of the way the game brings people together without hindrance because of race or colour or employment. There is a genuine mixing together without self-consciousness.

Consider the wives of All Blacks. Their men must go to training whether for club, province or country. They fly away overseas for months to play the sport they love and in the company of their friends. The wives are at home with the children. There is a longing to be where the husbands are, sharing, but unselfishly they give their men support and some have done it for six, eight, 10 years. It is not without danger to marriages — that has been shown. The wife who can no longer accept being, not herself, but the wife of an All Black — a sort of back-seat passenger — knows the danger if she says, "I can't cope, I miss you too much, the children need you, please give it up."

If I had to anticipate Murray playing rugby for another five years I couldn't take it. I'm glad I am not part of the bitterness which has pervaded rugby "wifedom" through the years. That is my good fortune. Given the circumstance that I had met Murray two or three years earlier than I did I could have been. Rugby has given me only good things. It has brought me into contact with people who have become my good friends. The image I had of the archetypal macho rugby player, big, rough, aggressive, was so far out. They play a hard, hard game but off the field I have found them to be mostly quiet, beautifully-mannered, gentle men.

Future fathomable

When Lorraine writes of the trend in recent years towards a more understanding administration, an administration more concerned for the players and their families, she touches a spot very close to every player's heart. Some administrators sense the need more acutely than others. When I captained one of the trial teams at Hamilton in 1984 the NZRFU councillor who was manager of the team distanced himself from the new players to the point of antagonising them. As the players arrived I took them into the house bar before dinner. As captain I encouraged this as a familiarisation exercise. The following morning the manager confronted me and said, "Right, the team spent $65 in the bar last night. We are going to close the house bar to the players." To me that worked out at something less than $4 a player and that seemed a bargain-basement price for the goodwill it engendered. So I told him it would be most unreasonable to close off the bar . . . "These are young guys and they're impressionable. It is their first exposure to the New Zealand Rugby Union. You must give them the opportunity to get together socially."

The reaction was that I was welcome to join him for a drink at any time but that he felt the team had "over-spent". I had already suggested to the players we have a post-match get-together with wives, girlfriends and a few invited guests. Perhaps, I said to the manager, I could arrange a room, a few chippies and peanuts, Bruce Smith and his stereo and tapes. And what if I bought a couple of cardboard cartons of wine and a couple of crates of flagon-beer? His response was a monumental expression of the very thing I had hoped our rugby administrators had left far behind them: "Well, you'll have to take the hat around."

I told him it was going to cost bugger-all and asked what sort of impression he was trying to give the kids. The Waikato Rugby Union liaison officer, Sid Green, suggested we ring Lion Breweries and ask for some beer and as it happened the Lion man, Tom Marinkovich, was delighted to help. He supplied eight dozen bottles. Following our training the manager came to me and said he would donate eight dozen to the team party. That seemed something of a coincidence. Later he announced to the team the beer had been donated by Lion and that he would give Hika Reid the money for our bottle store order. But by then it was too late. The image of rugby administration had been damaged again.

From the outset the manager had made it clear the New Zealand union would not be paying for laundry. That, of course, was ludicrous. Many of the players were going on to Rotorua for the North-South match; and, anyway, it shouldn't cost players a cent for laundry at a New Zealand trial.

It is necessary to expose this sort of event at a time when there is an increasing demand for a professional attitude to playing the game. While the players are under that demand there are still administrators who cannot keep in touch with the changing environment. It boils down to a need for administrators to have the pride in the game, the love of the game, the players have. If the administrators become so embroiled in bookwork and laws that they forget the human element of rugby then the game will not prosper.

I suggested to the union chairman, Ces Blazey, a year or so ago that there should be an annual dinner for councillors, the All Black team and their ladies. This would enable contact socially and only good could develop from it. At this late stage of my career I am only beginning to know some of the councillors — and I have to start all over again, anyway, because of the changes in the administration structure. For the first three years of my international career the bulk of the New Zealand administrators were merely names to me. Assuming we all have the same goal that makes no sense at all. The players must be conscious the administrators have their interests at heart but they must also be aware of the problems of the administrators.

The first player I heard slapping the wrist of rugby administrators was Dougie Rollerson, of Manawatu. Having just played on Athletic Park Dougie, who was never backward, noted in his after-match speech under the main grandstand that he had left his new wife "in the cupboard in the hallway" having cups of tea with other similarly disadvantaged wives while the chaps had their traditional session in a separate amenity. It made me think. I had not given great consideration to the

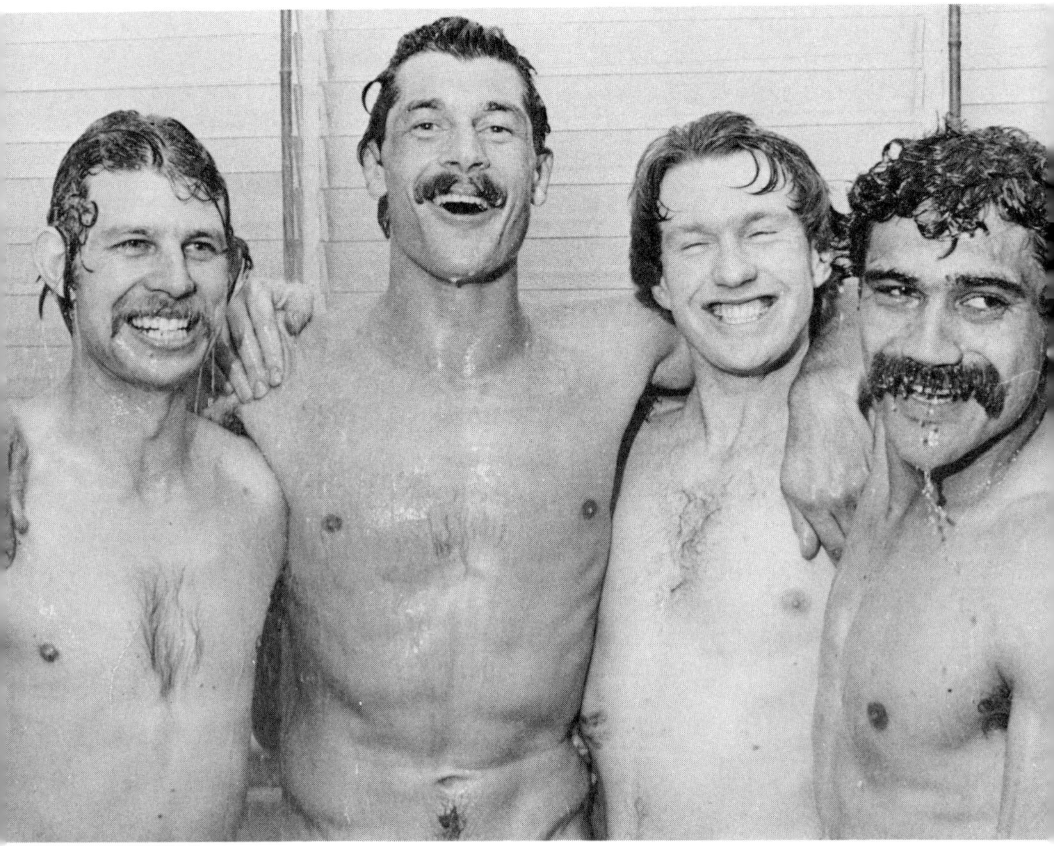

Nothing like a good, hot shower to unwind after a tough game. On this occasion, following Hewie's record-breaking 26 points against Australia at Eden Park, 1982, we Wellington guys had plenty to celebrate. That's Stu Wilson and Bernie Fraser making up the foursome.

women of rugby and their part in the game's social activities. Now I did. Why should the wives be rejected when they should be welcomed with open arms? That particular battle is not yet won but now there are enlightened men who have become close to the players and accept that women have an equal part to play in the game.

Women have changed, too, as they have set out to win equality. They have become part of a powerful social movement which will wear no part of being the little woman back home baking scones while her man hogs the headlines and the glory. As the demands on players have intensified so have the demands on their families and the demands of the women to have a part in their men's rugby lives. So they should be. So they **must** be.

There are for players certain basic essentials after a hard match. One of them is a hot shower. That being so you would assume that local rugby administrators would ensure that hot-water systems do not become so clapped-out that the players lack that simple amenity. Money is spent on many facilities for spectators — and for the administrators of the game, too. And it was uppermost in my mind that the administrators had let down the players again when I fired a scatter-gun of criticism at the Wellington Rugby Union in 1982. After a most difficult Ranfurly Shield match — a hard contest in bad conditions — the players went to the dressing rooms and the showers feeling as if they had been through the crusades. After a match I like to sit and just talk to the guy next to me or reflect quietly, let the rush go through, hop under the shower and luxuriate a little.

When you're steamed up, muscles aching a bit, mud in your hair, in your eyes, ears and nose, stinging from a scrape or two but happy to have come through with a narrow win the peasant rugby player asks little. A hot shower and a cold beer. Simplicity itself in this modern age. Sometimes the administrators do get confused and supply the beer hot and the shower cold. This was one of those days. And as the mud clung and the goose-bumps rose my patience trickled down the drain with the cold water. In my after-match speech I thanked the union for again providing the players with a cold shower as reward for a hard match played for the union's benefit. There was an almost audible raising of eyebrows, a flurry of whispered consternation — all of it in its way a reprimand for me rather than a confession of guilt. Afterward I was accosted by officials who considered I had taken rather much on myself. I told them the union had been aware for years of the shocking state of its hot-water system . . . "And today I have had a gutsful. The players have come second again. You've got your crowd and your gate and we've got cold showers."

The media sought the views of old players on what was seen to be my "outburst". Colin Meads said in his day they didn't complain about cold showers. I'm sure they didn't. But this was more than a decade after Pinetree and his stoical mates had taken their cold showers at Athletic Park and nothing had improved. Theirs was the era when All Blacks took everything the administrators chucked at them — the victims of that most outrageous of all administrative philosophies, "if you don't like it, you don't **have** to play." In our way current All Blacks are still pretty conservative . . . we don't exchange bunny-hugs and love-bites after a try is scored and we don't all get down on our hands and knees and kiss the ground when a test match has been won. But we do question matters which express an attitude detrimental to the players and we will not be patronised. Much ground has been made up in the general relationship between players and administrators and it has come about mainly through the initiative of the players themselves.

It was not some perverse mischief-making which brought about the great boot confrontation. For the first test against Australia in 1982 I wore Puma boots. Two days before the second test I was approached by an Adidas representative but I told him I wore the Pumas because they were fitted to the peculiarities of my feet — and till you have seen my bunions you don't know peculiar. I was told I was under contract to wear Adidas. I denied this, suggesting the New Zealand Rugby Union might be under contract but that my feet were my own . . . till Adidas had a personal contract with me I would not be wearing the product. As you would expect Adidas put pressure on the New Zealand Rugby Union who, in turn, put pressure on the players. I was approached by a council member and I told him my stand was based first on having Adidas and the union understand that players were people, too. I could appreciate the union wanting to have the gear-sponsorship Adidas offered but I doubted the compulsion placed on players to wear the boot. Nor were the players involved in any spin-off sportswear consideration. I received no money for wearing Puma as was obliquely suggested a couple of times but in my experience overseas Adidas, Puma, Coq Sportif offered "bonuses" of all sorts of sports equipment if you wore their product. In New Zealand I had found little eagerness even to replace unsatisfactory boots and it was extremely difficult to convince the suppliers that an exact fit was important.

The councillor was not happy — nor was he visibly impressed by the points I made. Andy Haden moved into the argument and decided mine was a worthy cause. So for the third test against Australia he joined me. He wore Laser. And Laser told us they would do everything in tailoring boots to individual foot peculiarities that Puma had done for me in South Africa. This fitted my principles. Not only would I be wearing a comfortable boot made for my foot but I would also be supporting a New Zealand-owned company — and I have always seen that to be important. So Andy and I wore Lasers and other players showed an interest in having boots made for their feet rather than just putting their feet into boots . . . Mark Shaw, Dave Loveridge, Bernie Fraser, Allan Hewson, Gary Whetton, Gary Knight, Steve Pokere . . .

At the time of the New Zealand trial in Hamilton in 1984 I wore

Laser. By the time we were in Rotorua for the North-South match the following Saturday there was an NZRFU edict: Wear Adidas or don't play for New Zealand. More words than that, but the meaning was clear. I wore Laser in the North-South.

Then before the first test against the French the same year we received in Christchurch another directive from the union. It was about as blunt as you could get. If we didn't wear Adidas boots in the first test we would not be selected for the second. We intended at first to call what we read as a bluff because we believed they had no right to dictate what we wore on our feet. We were amateur players in an amateur code. But then we decided the directive could have come only from people who were so pig-headed, so dogmatic, that they saw it as more important that the players toe the line than win the second test. There was in their attitude a great deal of tub-thumping — to the point, we felt, of irrationality. Cowboy Shaw has strange feet, too, so as a final gesture of defiance we demanded French-made Adidas caps, made of softer leather and much more comfortable. Eventually, these boots had to be courier-delivered from Sydney, courier-collected in Christchurch and, at a rough appraisal, cost about the equivalent of a pair of diamond-studded Italian fashion shoes.

So we wore the sponsor's product for the series. And so we conform. I am not decrying the boots. I am saying that I wear custom-made Lasers for all but New Zealand union matches.

In recent months there has been a rush of sponsorship for rugby in New Zealand. The blend Andy Haden, as the New Zealand Union's marketing consultant, has brought between the union's marketing committee and potential sponsors is a demonstration of his stature and his ability to deliver in the face of some pretty sulky criticism from within the union itself. It is also a demonstration of the marketable value of the game, and it emphasises that now that the commercialisation of the game is up and running the impetus must be maintained and increased by enlightened men coming through in administration. The game is running freely. It's a little like the All Blacks in the first spell of the second test against Argentina. The danger then was that we would close our minds and play the miserly game in the second spell. We did and to our great cost. The spate of commercial interest in rugby must now encourage inspired "selling" not constricting caution.

The game has come a long way since the whirlwind intrusion of David Lord and the megabucks nearly every All Black had mentally built his future on. For all the original complacency within the administra-

Spot the difference. In the 1981 picture (above) taken in France I'm playing in Adidas boots. Two years later against the Lions (below) I was operating in Lasers.

tion the time was right for that sort of revolution. The players had reached the point where the tortoise-pace of change in their conditions had ceased to be a matter of passing cynicism. I believe a political party once swept into power in New Zealand on the slogan, "It's time for a change." Well, that is how the top players of rugby in New Zealand felt. And when the right move came at that sensitively crucial time it was inevitable the players would move.

I was seen as one of the instigators of all that frantic activity which had Lord in New Zealand every second day, players signing statements of intent, meeting Lord in secrecy, holding clandestine meetings of their own. But when the Lord crusade was at its peak I was still in South Africa. When I came home that winter of 1983 I had not met, let alone spoken with David Lord. He was a name mixed up with a whole heap of dollar signs. But I must say the offer of a cool quarter million to fly high in the Lord circus sounded like a lot of fun. All the other members of the All Black team had drawn the same conclusion. Funtime. A great name for a quiz show, Fortune Funtime — provided you had all the answers and, regrettably, quizmaster Lord had not.

Had David Lord held more credibility with his backers I am sure the professional series would have happened. The professional circus was the right concept, the right timing, the wrong ringmaster. I will never be persuaded that David Lord, all unknowing, did not achieve in the space of a few weeks what the players could not achieve for themselves in the same number of years. Some administrators, at least, became aware that what Lord had tried and failed to do would be merely the opening gambit if they did not move to correct the grossly outdated expenses schedule for international players. At least now they were conscious that the players were not so enamoured of amateurism that they would lie down and allow themselves to be trampled roughshod for the sake of it. The amateur ideal is a worthy one. Its essential elements applied to rugby are one of the game's great attractions. But the definition of amateurism as meaning that the players of the game should accept being out of pocket and their jobs at risk to play it was the product of a dictionary of the bizarre.

Outside Lord there have been many approaches from rugby league through the years. I have discarded them first because I have little interest in league other than to take pleasure from the Kiwis international performances and I would never commit myself to playing any game from which I did not extract enjoyment. But nor did I want to be in the position of being contracted to a club, tied in without the freedom to move at the drop of a hat wherever I wished in the world . . . life at the drop of a hat: that has been what I have loved and which, for better or worse, has made me the person I am.

Much has been made of the "desertion" from tradition of moves to upmarket rugby and its accoutrements. The acceptance of the new fern has been seen as a fearful retreat from all that was near and dear to the hearts of All Blacks. I can understand the affection and the pride in which the fern is held because I, too, have worn it with no less pride than any of the critics of change. Were the new insignia some garbled, cheapjack version I would reject it. But, in fact, it is a graceful adornment to the black jersey. People outside rugby have been commercialising rugby for years. It seems to me high time rugby took its turn to gain benefit from its own game. These are marketing times and you cannot market unless you are promoting your product, whether it is a sport or a piece of merchandise.

Rugby has to be marketed as an entertainment and its return must be full value — and in New Zealand that is very substantial. I have experienced rugby in a country where the players are paid on a win/loss basis. I do not think that is good for the game because it creates undesirable sidelines — the bribing of players to throw a match or to remove an opponent considered to be dangerous to the desired result. These things happen in France and in spite of all the protestations at International Rugby Board level that they do not there is a bland acceptance in the country itself that they do.

However, I do believe that if you are creating a spectacle for public entertainment and which is earning a considerable sum of money the players should benefit from it in some form.

There is a fine line between commercialism and professionalism. It is really just the manner in which revenue is distributed or the manner in which a player may earn for his contribution to the game. People cannot expect players who have the talent to be at the top to give the game their dedication and to make the sacrifices (of which in the modern game there are many) yet be out of pocket at the end of the day. That does not mean direct payment to players on the win/loss system. Players should be free to market themselves off the field. That is a process which spins off directly to the benefit of the game. If a player achieves sufficient profile to be seen as a marketing proposition he should be free to get out there and endorse like crazy. Every time he is seen on television or in a newspaper or magazine advertisement he is prompting thousands and thousands of viewers — and especially the kids — to relate him to the game. He is giving the sport mileage with every pair of briefs, every computer, every can of juice he wears, punches or swallows. Every commercial becomes a commercial for rugby. When Colin Meads carries fenceposts or Andy Haden blesses a brand of personal computer "rugby" is in the viewer's mind.

New Zealand is wakening to it. And that may make it easier for me to make people understand why through the years I have been coming home from overseas "so late" as they put it. What could I say when I was leaving the equivalent of $1000 a week net for playing rugby and working in the promotional field for a commercial company, living on a beautiful beach with good surf to return to training in a cold southerly, showering under lukewarm-to-cold water and paying to have my gear laundered every week? The fact is, however, that I **did** return — and without reservation.

I want to be a part of the exciting future of rugby, to go with it into the market place, maintaining its high profile with the changing demands of society. I have written of my first sharp impressions of rugby in the sawdust gym at Tawa with my father coaching a second division team and, after the game, the players and supporters shuffling in the sawdust as they poured their beer from flagons and snacked on water biscuits and mild cheddar. And not a woman in sight. Twenty years on we have sophisticated club rooms, finely carpeted and furnished, a bar with all mod-cons and women as much a part of the scene as their men. Twenty years from now the social activities of rugby as we know them will not satisfy young people. That is where thought must be turned now. The game's broad base of multi-religious, multi-ethnic, multi-social membership will not change but there will be different demands from different social groups and rugby must be prepared to move with that flow.

Consider Athletic Park. It has been a great ground to me and I love it even after a muddy southerly and a cold shower. It is my home ground and I like to think it is the centrepiece of New Zealand rugby. When I was a kid clambering to the top deck of the Millard Stand and looking down at the chess game unfolding far below it was like watching rugby from heaven. To hold its status as a fine international stadium Athletic Park will need covered accommodation in its full sweep — and that does not mean the end of seating for mum, dad and the kids from every walk of life. They **are** rugby.

I can envisage an Athletic Park with viewing-suites at the periphery, surrounding the playing area, suites leased or sold to companies to extend hospitality to their clients. Already tennis has moved far ahead of the field in this in New Zealand and that comes from clear administrative foresight. But for rugby the transition would be on a much big-

Andy Haden and Graham Mourie, two All Blacks now helping to market the game, here show off their bilingual skills during a tour of France.

ger and more permanent scale. At Ellis Park, Johannesburg, where they have multi-racial soccer, multi-racial boxing, super-multi-racial rock concerts, private hospitality suites surround the ground in two levels. They are leased to private companies, public companies, commercial organisations of all sorts, even to individuals. As the entertainment spreads out before them 20 guests or so in each suite watch it at their ease — snacks, drinks, telephone, easy access to car parks. Out of sight? Of course it is. So it was in Johannesburg a handful of years ago. But not out of mind. As international rugby goes into its World Cup era so must the game's ego move with it.

I want to turn my energies and my ideas to that end, for the game as a whole rather than for team or club. It is the format of the future and I feel it as an exciting venture to be involved in. The turn of the wheel will bring advantages to everyone . . . income from the suites turned to extended facilities for general public whether at Athletic Park, Eden Park, Lancaster and Carisbrook and within the scope, too, of the provincial grounds.

I hope I have set in train for my own club a series of events which will be a model for other clubs to follow. In 1985 our senior team was raising funds to go on tour — whether to Argentina or to South Africa — and part of the exercise was, inevitably, the working bee. I was conscious that I could not give the time to that sort of fundraising so I sought another avenue: one major event to short-circuit the house-painting, rubbish collection, lawn-mowing, demolition scene. During training one evening when I should have been thinking of some matchless tactic to win Saturday's game I considered instead "the grand project". What was the most controversial issue of the day? Who had the highest profile within it? Answers in sequence: the All Black tour of South Africa. The All Blacks and John Minto.

Something, then, involving tour, All Black, Minto. I tumbled it about after training and came up with a great luncheon meeting at the Michael Fowler Centre. John Minto to present his case. I to present the All Blacks'. Rob Muldoon to chair the show. That got me a big laugh. It couldn't be done. It **could** be done and it **would** be. The idea of having John Minto as a guest speaker to a rugby club was going to create immense interest. But would he come? Alan Muir's letter to him noted that within rugby itself there was division on whether the tour should go ahead. Our club was no exception to that and many players would be intensely interested in hearing his point of view. I would respond with mine. Minto agreed. Muldoon agreed. Mexted would be there — the day of the three Ms was at hand.

The day of the three Ms — Minto, Muldoon, Mexted. Here we are after our exchange of views at the highly successful Wellington Football Club luncheon. Between Sir Robert and myself is Barry Evans, WFC president.

And it was a huge success. John Minto was given a reception he might never have dreamed possible from an audience of rugby-lovers. Sir Rob allowed no bias to insinuate itself into his chairmanship — low-key Sir Rob, this. I thanked John for being a part of our fund-raising campaign and it was only then, I think, that he realised it had been organised for that purpose. He was not impressed. Well, he wouldn't be, would he? There was no malice in it though, on reflection, we did find it wryly bizarre. And a worthwhile charity, too — the Wellington Football Club's travelling fund.

But the tour did not go ahead. So what to do with the thousands of dollars? I proposed it should be put into a property: This is the day of incentive-facilities for players so buy a pretty rough house in a close suburb, say Newtown, and with club-member expertise renovate it. Have a student member of the club living in it at all times but with the house thrown open as a residence for new players coming into the club from outside Wellington.

Let this happen in the first year then sell. Buy a better house. And then a better house. By the end of three or four years our club house is a fine home with a spa pool. After ten years it is an establishment with a gymnasium, a full pool and a tennis court — and a great incentive for new players at a nominal rental.

This will happen if club members have the vision to give it a go. The possibilities are endless. Eventually, the club may have a lease on a hotel as an accommodation house for rugby . . .

Rugby has **everywhere** to go in New Zealand. It deserves the best shot of every person who claims allegiance to it. In my own playing years rugby has given me the scope to live my life as I have wanted to live it. It can give that same opportunity to others, to thousands upon thousands of others, but at the end of the day the player who does not turn back to the game to thank it and to regenerate it with his gratitude has achieved less than nothing, for he is truly unfulfilled.

There is no place in the game for the half-hearted for they apply the brakes to the full-spirited upon whom the game's destiny depends. Einstein, with a little help from Andy Haden, says it again: "Great spirits have always encountered violent opposition from mediocre minds."

That is the battle rugby must win.

MEXTED — No 8
a pictorial essay

The tactic in action. Third test, Wallabies, 1982. Commit their loosies and inside backs — Chris Roche, Michael Hawker (tackling), Phillip Cox — clear it and move it. This picture by Bob Tulloch of Tauranga won a top award at the New Zealand professional photographers national show. Title: Black Power.

Hang on! About to swallow a Laidlaw clearance v Lions, 1983.

Not a bad throw, Andy . . . or am I quite high enough? Cardiff, Arms Park, 1980.

No surfboard, no wet-suit but still surfing . . . Carisbrook v Lions, 1983.

All Black trial and typical support from Bruce Middleton who appeared the logical successor to Graham Mourie.

In possession and ready to threaten anyone obstructing my path.

Scrum clearance to Loveridge under pressure from Lions halfback Roy Laidlaw. John O'Driscoll hovers. Fourth test, 1983.

The two of us . . . Jean-luc Joinel and me. Objectives: similar. Wellington v France, 1984.

Crunchtime coming up. Lions, 1983.

Text-book tactics against a short lineout opponent . . . Ross Reynolds can feel my left hand but Roger Quittenton can't see it.

It's easy to look good against average opposition . . . v Canada, 1980.

Typical Shaw body-position — head down and driving against the Lions, 1983. Jeff Squire observes.

Three Wallabies committed and the ball still available . . . Simon Poidevin, Peter Lucas and David Campese.

1979 — first test, first try. Scotland and, appropriately, Murrayfield. Defence of Alan Lawson and John Rutherford too late and Andy Dalton in support.

Help, Jock! I need you — Australia, Sydney, 1984, Mark Ella at ankles, James Black at waist, Chris Roche and Ross Reynolds select their portion.

Down, but not out. Ensuring the move doesn't die against the Lions in 1983.

Canada, 1980. Haden not required on voyage.

Looking Mark Ella dead in the eye during the 1982 series. Wayne Smith is champing to become involved.

Postscript ...

Rugby player — or rebel?

I write this from Bloemfontein, without regret, without apology. I believe in what the media are pleased to call the rebel tour of South Africa. I am in good company: 29 other players, a coach who was the greatest All Black, a manager who played 38 consecutive test matches . . . and, I have just heard, with the support of 78 per cent of New Zealanders polled by the country's biggest-circulating weekly newspaper. With that sort of support can it be said with sincerity that we are damaging New Zealand rugby?

We have just beaten Orange Free State 31-9 after taking one-point victories from the badly-named "Junior" Springboks and from that team which epitomises the Afrikaner physically and mentally — Northern Transvaal. We are learning what it means to play rugby as New Zealanders in this country where rugby is a test match no matter the name of the opposition, no matter the day of the week. Though I have played rugby here at provincial level I number myself among the learners. Though I have understanding of the mentality and the physical toughness of the South African rugby man I, too, am astonished by the incessant demand to contest and combat. Rugby on this tour exposes rugby players, their strengths and weaknesses, their skills and lack of skills. Rugby on the high veldt, the lungs screaming for more air, the throat burning-dry, the ground like flint, the opposition like teak. The challenge is the inspiration. You rise to it or you fall by the wayside.

So why are we here? Is it only because we have always harboured the desire to play the Springboks in South Africa and to beat them? Reason enough, but not all the reason. We are here because to a man we believe we have the right to be here, to play sport or to travel where ever, as individuals, we wish. Most of the players feel strongly that by some odd quirk of the law something which was rightfully theirs to choose was snatched from them on July 13, 1985. They could not then and still cannot understand how that could be construed as justice.

When the programmed tour was cancelled last year and then the unofficial tour aborted there was no lessening of desire to take our rugby on to South African grounds. Probably the reverse. There was a hardening of resolve and it was inevitable that this would find expression.

We knew we could not go to South Africa as a team under the banner of the New Zealand Rugby Union. Nor, we believed, should we expect any sanction of the union, nor apply to it for dispensation as a team to play in South Africa. The motivation for this was not fear for ourselves but concern for any embarrassment to the New Zealand union. I have written in an earlier chapter that the game of rugby must not be abused by circumstance or design. I reaffirm that now. Not one player on this tour — and assuredly not Colin Meads or Ian Kirkpatrick — believes rugby the game will take harm in New Zealand from it.

The Transvaal Rugby Union, working through an Auckland businessman named Winston McDonald, affirmed every player who had been selected for the original tour was eager to take part in this one. At the beginning I am sure both John Kirwan and David Kirk were to be a part of it. The senior players from north, central and south were invited to act as liaison in their areas and it was my job to organise players in the lower half of the North Island.

It was the work not of weeks but of months to tidy up the organisation. The legal representative of the Transvaal Rugby Union, Mervyn Key, travelled through New Zealand and met every player individually. The players took legal counsel from Shane Treadwell, a Wellington lawyer, and with him discussed the broadest aspects of their intent and the possible consequences of it. Perhaps the most difficult facet of our plan was that we could not take into our confidence our own club and provincial coaches. We were aware we would come under criticism for this and were sensitive to the difficulties it might cause.

It gives me great satisfaction to learn from New Zealand that the absence of established All Blacks from the provincial teams has, in fact, created a new base for selectors and that they and their players have risen to an unexpected challenge. I was delighted to receive news of Wellington's successes against New South Wales and Fiji.

Secrecy was all-important. We all had experience of the pressures placed on families through suggestion of involvement with South Africa and we were resolved it must not happen here. The story did break, of course, a couple of weeks before we left but there was still sufficient doubt about it for players to reject it or decline to comment on it. This

Dejected Cavaliers captain Andy Dalton after Geldenhuys' punch had broken his jaw in Pretoria.

led to some searing charges of dishonesty. Everyone who has never lied in his life leaped on to that bandwagon. Notable among them were politicians!

One newspaper ran a headline which claimed Colin Meads had denied all knowledge of a tour but at no part of the story under it was Meads quoted as saying that at all.

I was asked several times whether I had received an invitation to go on a rebel tour of South Africa. I said I had not. I still have not. There was assumption that those of us who played in the International Rugby Board centennial matches in Wales and England would return through South Africa to play in composite world teams. There were no such invitations. That may seem to be academic and that as I was working to organise the players in my area to go to South Africa I was, tacitly at least, invited. Maybe. I answered the question that was put to me. No more. There was no way any player was going to place his loved ones under the mindless attention of the "pure" people who use the telephone to terrorise women and children.

The guts of the whole thing is that we wanted to play rugby on tour in South Africa. It had been stated categorically at the time of the court injunction that there was nothing to stop All Blacks going to South Africa as individuals, linking up there and playing rugby — though not as the representatives of the New Zealand Rugby Union. As I have recorded, the Prime Minister himself said as much.

So each of us applied for a visa through the South African consulate in Sydney, received it, and went to South Africa. We were quite clear that as New Zealanders we were free to travel whereever we chose. Of course we considered repercussions. Less than a year before, the New Zealand Rugby Union had voted strongly in favour of touring South Africa. We have now achieved that — though not on the union's behalf. We have accepted the responsibility. The tour could not otherwise have happened.

I asked Colin Meads whether he had considered the penalty he as a New Zealand selector might be called upon to pay. He said, "Yes. But what we have done is keep open a door which should never have been closed in rugby. I have been prepared to make the sacrifice of my All Black selection job, if that should be necessary, to keep the door open."

Some of the reaction took us by surprise. We were a little taken aback by the vehemence of Ces Blazey's condemnation, but not surprised at all by David Lange's. When the Sport Minister, Mike Moore, used Anzac Day and the sacrifice of the heroes of Gallipoli to condemn us

The combination that had served New Zealand since 1979, still going strong in South Africa in 1986 — Trapper Loveridge and me ·

Wayne Smith attacking against Northern Transvaal at Loftus Versfeld, chased by Johan Spangenberg. Gary Whetton is in support.

there was anger that he could so distort the issue to make that sort of flamboyant capital. He might as easily have said that the heroes of Gallipoli fought for precisely the sort of freedom we had exercised.

The team released this statement to the press when we gathered in South Africa: "Our team members have been invited by the Transvaal Rugby Union to play in South Africa as a collection of individual players. We are not the All Blacks. That is the official team of the New Zealand Rugby Union. We will be known as the Cavaliers. We are aware South Africa has political problems but as sportsmen we emphasise it would be improper for us to comment on them. We are here to play sport and will not at any stage debate politics or answer politically-slanted

One try was enough to beat Northern Transvaal, and here it comes as Mike Clamp goes around Johan Heunis.

questions. We will be playing 12 games, four of which will be against a South African team. These will not be official tests as we do not represent an official rugby union or the NZRFU . . . at no stage of the tour will team members talk to the media . . ."

The last thing anyone wanted of this tour was that it should jeopardise the careers of a large percentage of the players. I have been most concerned about the future of the younger players, the preservation of their status. It has been said repeatedly that the players on tour are receiving allowances aligned with those prescribed by the International Rugby Board. It is true that commercial oportunities have existed in South Africa to a wider extent than on most tours — the sale of tickets allocated to the team brings a more urgent response than anywhere else in the world and the team "pool" grows accordingly. This is no more than what has been experienced by all international teams touring South Africa. No one was talked into this tour. Each player could say "yes" or "no" and that would be the end of it. Everyone was aware there could be repercussions and there was acceptance of that situation.

But no one expected to be banned.

When Danie Craven finally announced the South African Rugby Board's support for the tour I believe he was saying, in effect, "We have nowhere to go. The International Rugby Board has told us to exert influence to have the tour discontinued. We will not do that and if this means our disqualification as a member of the board then so be it. If, as a sporting organisation which has striven to achieve integration in our sport — sometimes outside the laws of the land — we are now to be penalised by our international body then we will make our own way."

I see that as a direct forerunner to more tours of the sort we have undertaken. South Africa is not going to accept isolation in its rugby. It has seen the effects of isolation in other sports and it has seen sports people from many countries in the world come to South Africa to compete without penalty or threat from other African countries. The Afrikaner is stubborn to the point of pig-headedness. He can be narrow-minded and objectionable. The Voortrekker toughness is in his rugby as it is in his character. One day after training at Loftus Versfeld for the Northern Transvaal match I insisted on taking the boys to the Voortrekker Monument because it encapsulates the nature of the Boer. He has fought desperately to maintain a hold on the land and the women and children fought and died with him. He was pushed, fighting all the way, from the coast to the high veldt and there he said, thus far and no further. He has not changed. I wanted the young players to understand that what the Afrikaner was then he still is and that is what makes him the most difficult, the most formidable rugby opponent of all. Within his predictability there is such toughness that being able to read his intent is only a fraction of the battle won.

Everyone was pleased to hear of Ces Blazey's confidence that next year's World Cup will proceed as planned and of his refusal to be harrassed into premature judgement of the players in South Africa. There has been a strong movement toward moral judgement of us yet not of the New Zealand body-builders' team whose intention to come to South Africa became public about the same time. Essentially, the principle is the same whether we are playing before 50,000 or the body-

Grant Fox attacking. It was his goalkicking, though, that was to be a critical factor on the Cavaliers tour.

builders competing before 1000.

As I write this we contemplate our captain Andy Dalton having been taken out of the tour with a double fracture of the jaw, the work of Burger Geldenhuys who was unrepentant about it all. After the match against Northern Transvaal I asked Geldenhuys whether he had been responsible for hitting Andy from behind. He said he had and with

Scott Crichton seems determined to wrench Tollie Oosthuizen's head off during the Northern Transvaal game, which the Cavaliers won 10-9.

that he lost my respect. It was interesting to see the Afrikaner press leap to the defence of the Northern front row which was twice cautioned by the referee. *Die Beeld* found that it was the New Zealand front row which had openly antagonised its opponents and which should have been warned. It was an assessment based on blind nationalism.

The end of Dalton's tour and, probably, his career was tragic. He has won the highest esteem among rugby people for his fairness and even temper. Without his integrity the tour probably would not have happened and that he should have been removed from it so abruptly was a desperate disappointment to the team. It did not sour the tour; it bought yet more resolution.

The defeat of Northern Transvaal so early in the tour and in the rarified atmosphere of Pretoria was significant. The rolling of Orange Free State at Bloemfontein by an outstanding team performance was, to some extent, the sort of result I predicted "would have been" had the official All Black tour taken place.

What eventuated on the rest of the tour is now history, of course, but Colin Meads was under no misapprehension of the difficulty we would have. He said, "They're better than I thought they'd be, specially up front where I thought we'd have them. It's going to be a long, hard road."

The first game straightened out any misconceptions among the players about 60-point midweek wins in Argentina. That looked good in the books and in its context it was good. But related to South Africa it meant nothing and it was as well the players came to understand that

Defeating Northern Transvaal was significant. Here Vic Simpson is shadowed by Northerns' goalkicking whizz Naas Botha.

in the very first game. It may be there was some sort of blessing, after all, in the most rigorous itinerary any team in history has undertaken. I see the itinerary as a deliberate attempt to set-up the team for a thorough pasting in the "tests". Originally there were to be only three "tests". A fourth enabled the organisers to play another match at Ellis Park and there was pressure to have us play it and alleviate to some extent the fierce indebtedness of the Transvaal Rugby Union.

The players found it difficult to accept that the television authorities in New Zealand decreed the public should not watch the matches because they were unofficial and, therefore, "irrelevant". The judgement by television people of what in sport is relevant has often been a matter of high comedy. We learned of the television decision at the same time as we picked up the results of the newspaper poll. I'm not sure who exactly judges for New Zealanders what they want to view. I would have thought that of substantial relevance would have been the attitude of the New Zealand public. But as with many things in our absorbent society the public appeared not to be considered. There was a self-righteousness about the decision, a tunnel-visioned element which, dare I say it, I would more have expected to find in deep Afrikanerdom.

The atmosphere within the team on tour has been unaffected by anything which may be at the end of it. It became clear during the Argentina experience that there was a great feel about the team and among the players. In South Africa it has been an even closer unit. There is stimulation in the challenge and determination to hold team discipline at the highest level. There is understanding that in any environment of great hospitality there is increased responsibility.

There are no illusions about some of the hospitality. Decidedly motivated by other than concern that we should always be at peak to perform on the field. We started with a physiotherapist but no masseur on a tour which for six weeks was going to put the body through hell. We demanded a masseur. She arrived wearing a highly-cut leotard and a lowly-cut neckline. A masseuse. And distracting. Socially, they want to buy you ten drinks, not one. You want to be home and in bed by 11 pm; they set out to ensure it will not be till 3am.

No illusions. They know what we have risked to get to South Africa, but they set out to destroy us. And we would not have it otherwise. Before he left New Zealand, Colin Meads made the point . . . "We are going there to win. That is what this tour and all tours are about."

As I write this, the spirit to achieve that is truly alight in a team of players who determined to tour South Africa because it was their right.

Statistics

Murray Mexted made his first class rugby debut for a Wellington B selection against Marlborough at Blenheim on June 2, 1975. He played twice more that year for B teams, against Horowhenua at Levin and Nelson Bays at Motueka.

He played for a Wellington XV against Wanganui at Wanganui on May 12, 1976 and for the same selection against New Zealand Marist at Wellington on May 16 that year.

Till the end of 1985, Mexted had played 114 games at first class level for the province, 109 of them for A teams.

His A team debut was against Wairarapa-Bush at Masterton on June 1, 1976.

Mexted has scored 24 tries for his province, the first being against Horowhenua at Levin in 1981 when Wellington won 56-6.

Mexted's try-scoring for Wellington followed an interesting pattern, probably due in part to rules of the day and tactical approaches by the various Wellington teams. After scoring his first try in 1981 he added two more that year, five more in 1982, five again in 1983 and 10, including a hat trick against Hawke's Bay, in 1984.

In 1985, Mexted scored only one try for the province.

His yearly appearances for Wellington were:

1975 3 (Wellington B)
1976 17 (including two for Wellington XVs, and 15 for A teams).
1977 8.
1978 9.
1979 10.
1980 6.
1981 13.
1982 15.
1983 10.
1984 13.
1985 10.

Murray Mexted has played 71 matches for the All Blacks, including 34 consecutive official tests, since his debut in the first of two unoffical tests against Argentina in 1979.

He has represented New Zealand in 11 countries, including New Zealand.

Mexted played in 59 winning All Black teams, experiencing defeat eight times. He was also involved in four draws.

He has scored 19 tries for New Zealand teams, his first being against London Division at Twickenham in 1979. His first test try was in his debut as a test player against Scotland at Murrayfield, also in 1979. Mexted has also scored test tries against Australia (at Christchurch in 1982) and against England (at Wellington in 1985).

MURRAY MEXTED'S RECORD AS AN ALL BLACK

1979	v Argentina at Dunedin (unofficial test)	won 18-9	
	v Argentina at Wellington (unofficial test)	won 15-6	
	v London Division at Twickenham	won 21-18	1 try
	v South of Scotland at Hawick	won 19-3	
	v Midland Division at Leicester	won 33-3	1 try
	v Glasgow at Glasgow	won 12-6	
	v Scotland at Murrayfield	won 20-6	1 try
	v Northern Division at Otley	lost 9-21	
	v South & South West Counties at Exeter	won 16-0	
	v England at Twickenham	won 10-9	
1980	v Sydney at Sydney	drew 13-13	
	v South Australia at Adelaide	won 75-3	1 try
	v Victoria at Melbourne	won 45-6	1 try
	v New South Wales at Sydney	won 12-4	
	v New South wales Country at Newcastle	won 34-3	
	v Australia at Sydney	lost 9-13	
	v Australia at Brisbane	won 12-9	
	v Australian Universities at Brisbane	won 33-3	
	v Australia at Sydney	lost 10-26	
	v Nadroga at Lautoka	won 14-6	
	v Suva at Suva	won 33-4	
	v Fiji at Suva	won 30-6	
	v Canada at Vancouver	won 43-10	
	v Cardiff at Cardiff	won 16-9	
	v Swansea at Swansea	won 32-0	
	v Newport at Newport	won 14-3	
	v Wales at Cardiff	won 23-3	
1981	v Scotland at Dunedin	won 11-4	
	v Scotland at Auckland	won 40-15	

	v South Africa at Christchurch	won 14-9	
	v South Africa at Wellington	lost 12-24	
	v South Africa at Auckland	won 25-22	
	v Romania at Bucharest	won 14-6	
	v Languedoc-Roussillion XV at Perpignan	drew 6-6	
	v France at Toulouse	won 13-9	
	v France at Paris	won 18-6	
1982	v Australia at Christchurch	won 23-16	1 try
	v Australia at Wellington	lost 16-19	
	v Australia at Auckland	won 33-18	
1983	v British Isles at Christchurch	won 16-12	
	v British Isles at Wellington	won 9-0	
	v British Isles at Dunedin	won 15-8	
	v British Isles at Auckland	won 38-6	
	v Australia at Sydney	won 18-8	
	v South of Scotland at Galashiels	won 30-9	
	v Northern Division at Gateshead	won 27-21	
	v Midland Division at Leicester	lost 13-19	
	v Scotland at Murrayfield	drew 25-25	
	v South & South West Division at Bristol	won 18-6	
	v England at Twickenham	lost 9-15	
1984	v France at Christchurch	won 10-9	
	v France at Auckland	won 31-18	
	v Queensland B at Brisbane	won 37-0	2 tries
	v New South Wales at Sydney	won 37-10	
	v South Australia at Adelaide	won 99-0	1 try
	v Victoria at Melbourne	won 65-3	2 tries
	v Australia at Sydney	lost 9-16	
	v Sydney at Sydney	won 28-3	1 try
	v New South Wales Country at Tamworth	won 21-3	1 try
	v Australia at Brisbane	won 19-15	
	v New South Wales B at Gosford	won 21-15	
	v Australia at Sydney	won 25-24	
	v Eastern XV at Suva	won 58-0	2 tries
	v Fiji at Suva	won 45-0	1 try
1985	v England at Christchurch	won 18-13	
	v England at Wellington	won 42-15	1 try
	v Australia at Auckland	won 10-9	
	v Rosario at Rosario	won 28-9	1 try
	v Buenos Aires XV at Buenos Aires	won 31-13	1 try
	v Argentina at Buenos Aires	won 33-20	
	v Argentina at Buenos Aires	drew 21-21	

Cavalier in name but not in approach, on the playing fields of South Africa, 1986.

Mexted played in All Black trial matches in 1977 (at Wanganui), 1979 (at Pukekohe), 1980 (at Hamilton), 1983 (at Wellington) and 1984 (at Hamilton). He represented the North Island in the annual inter-island clash in 1978 (at New Plymouth), 1979 (at Invercargill), 1980 (at Palmerston North) and 1984 (at Rotorua). Mexted was selected for the 1985 North Island team at New Plymouth and subsequently was made captain, but he was forced to withdraw with injury.